GREAT COURTROOM
LAWYERS

A M E R I C A N
P R O F I L E S

GREAT COURTROOM LAWYERS

Fighting the Cases That Made History

■

Marian Calabro

☑®
Facts On File, Inc.
AN INFOBASE HOLDINGS COMPANY

Great Courtroom Lawyers: Fighting the Cases That Made History

Copyright © 1996 by Marian Calabro

Facts On File, Inc.
11 Penn Plaza
New York NY 10001

Library of Congress Cataloging-in-Publication Data

Calabro, Marian.
    Great courtroom lawyers : fighting the cases that made history /
Marian Calabro.
        p. cm.— (American profiles)
    Includes bibliographical references and index.
    ISBN 0-8160-3323-4 (acid-free paper)
    1. Lawyers—United States—Biography. I. Title. II. Series:
American profiles (Facts On File, Inc.)
KF372.C35 1996
349.73′092—dc20
[B]
[347.30092]
[B]   96-5107

Text design by Ron Monteleone

Cover design by Matt Galemmo

Printed in the United States of America

MP FOF 10 9 8 7 6 5 4 3 2 1

This book is printed on acid-free paper.

Contents

Acknowledgments

I thank Linda Fairstein, Sarah Weddington, F. Lee Bailey, and the late William Kunstler for their time and courtesy in providing interviews and/or photographs for this book.

For insights into corporate law, trial law, and military law, respectively, I thank John Rousmaniere, Fred Bennett, and Art Sevigny. Special appreciation goes to my research assistant, Katherine Kirkpatrick; to the public librarians of Bergen County, New Jersey, especially those in Hasbrouck Heights and Fair Lawn; and to Bernie Libster, for being there.

Introduction

Help wanted. Must have a flair for the dramatic. Must also be able to withstand pressure, long hours, possible death threats. Persuasive style essential. Knowledge of rules of evidence a must. Ongoing interest in truth and justice a plus. Good pay, unless you work for the government.

*B*ecoming a courtroom attorney is a career each lawyer forges for him/herself. Each path is different, as the nine profiles in this book illustrate. There are no employment ads for litigators like the imaginary one above. The basic course of study leads just as easily to tamer legal specialties like tax law or trademark work.

Yet when we think of lawyers, we envision them not behind desks but on their feet in the halls of justice. We picture F. Lee Bailey lacing into defiant witnesses like Mark Fuhrman in the O. J. Simpson case. We see Clarence Darrow in a dusty southern town, cajoling a jury to allow John Scopes to teach evolution. We picture William Kunstler leaping up to cry "medieval torture!" when the judge orders a rebellious Chicago Seven defendant to be gagged and tied to his chair.

The images continue. There is Belva Lockwood, pedaling her bicycle to court to win reparations for Civil War veterans and Cherokee Indians; John W. Davis, eloquently representing captains of industry and making a last stand for segregated schools; Robert H. Jackson, doggedly cross-examining Hitler's henchmen after World War II; Linda Fairstein, persuasively requesting maximum jail time for convicted rapists.

When issues are so big or controversial that only the Supreme Court can decide them, we see Thurgood Marshall culminating his long crusade against "separate but equal" education, or Sarah Weddington arguing for abortion rights. It's no accident that both of these landmark cases had to be presented twice; sometimes even the highest court in the land needs extra time to hear arguments and decide on them.

Increasingly, we picture courtroom lawyers on television. Broadcasts of trials began as experiments in the 1980s, and became round-the-clock drama with Court TV. The nine-month–long spectacle of *California v. Orenthal James Simpson* renewed debate about the role of cameras in the courtroom. Do televised trials educate the public about its legal system? Or do they turn lawyers into ham actors, and summations into sound bites? Similar questions were asked about radio coverage of sensational trials earlier in the century. When Clarence Darrow defended teenage "thrill killers" Leopold and Loeb, listeners across the country clamored to have the hearings broadcast on radio, but the judge refused.

By order of the United States Congress, no federal trial can be televised. Therefore, crimes against the government—like the 1995 bombing of the Alfred P. Murrah Federal Building in Oklahoma City—cannot, in theory, become grist for media spectacles. The ban also means that viewers will never see the Supreme Court in action. Visitors to Washington, D.C., however, can wait on line for free tickets when Court is in session. Entering those hushed chambers and witnessing the justices in action is an experience well worth the trip.

Lawyers' zeal for publicity is nothing new. After representing himself in court in ancient Greece, the philosopher Socrates took to the streets of Athens to explain himself and his case. Was he different from the many lawyers in this book who have held press conferences on courthouse steps or gone on the lecture circuit to promote their ideas?

Legal dramas have always found ready audiences. From Aristotle to William Shakespeare to John Grisham, writers have spun classic entertainments from courtroom conflicts. Most of the people and cases in this book have been else-where dramatized or fictionalized; just search by name or subject in any library or video store to find them.

DNA testing will probably affect trials more than television will. In trying to prove guilt "beyond a reasonable doubt," as they must, prosecutors have progressed far past lie detector tests—a bulwark of F. Lee Bailey's early career—and finger-prints. Positive DNA identification, based on body products such as hair or semen, can link a suspect to a crime scene more definitively than anything else. But while DNA tests have an error rate of 1 in 57 million, they do not guarantee a quick trial or sure verdict, as evidenced by the cases of O. J. Simpson or the Central Park jogger.

Market research is another new factor in courtrooms. In big cases, lawyers now employ jury selection consultants. Each side in a trial has a certain number of peremptory chal-lenges, or vetoes, based on the severity of the charge. Although jurors should be deciding cases on evidence and testimony, statistics show that one-third of them decide dur-ing opening arguments! Consultants help lawyers determine who may fit that pattern, since such a person may become a holdout and create a hung jury, which requires a new trial.

"Some people never change their minds after deciding some-thing—are you like that?" they may ask a candidate. Clarence Darrow, a master at selecting juries, relied on instinct in such matters. Thurgood Marshall generally accepted the first 12 jurors and trusted them to do their job. "You can never tell what's on somebody's mind," Marshall found.

In the end, a trial is a "contest of credibility," rather than a pure search for truth, as author/lawyer Timothy Sullivan points out in his book *Unequal Verdicts: The Central Park Jogger Trials.* "The winner of the contest is the lawyer who convinces a jury that his interpretation of the evidence makes more sense that of his opponent," Sullivan writes. "In many cases, what may or may not have actually happened will never objectively be known."

Many criminal defense lawyers don't know if their clients are guilty, and don't want to know. Ron Kuby, the law partner and successor to William Kunstler, says: "When lawyers sit down and sketch out possible defenses with their clients, they ask 'Is this believable?' And only then [if at all] do you engage in the question 'Is it true?'" Fred Bennett, a Legal Aid Society lawyer who represents poor and indigent suspects in New York City, adds: "Often we focus more on the prosecution's case than on what clients tell us."

People often wonder how attorneys can bring themselves to defend rapists, spouse murderers, terrorist bombers, and other heinous criminals. Broadly speaking, that duty is part of every lawyer's job description. Because suspects in the United States are innocent until proven guilty, the court is under the obligation to provide every accused person with a lawyer.

This system of justice goes back to the U.S. Constitution. Suspects' rights are embedded in the Sixth Amendment, which establishes the right to "a speedy and public trial" by jury, and in this crucial phrase from the Fourteenth Amendment: "nor shall any state deprive any person of life, liberty, or property, without due process of law, nor deny to any person within its jurisdiction the equal protection of the laws."

Still, finding counsel for certain suspects is not easy. For example, the process took weeks in the case of Oklahoma City bombing suspect Timothy McVeigh. The man who finally took the job, Stephen Jones, told National Public Radio: "Criminal defense lawyers are to the legal profession what proctologists are to the medical profession—necessary but not desirable."

Lawyers as a group have never been well-loved. This line from Shakespeare's *Henry VI, Part 2* is still quoted: "The first thing we do, let's kill all the lawyers." Some 400 years later, such sentiments take the form of jokes such as the two following: What would you call 6,000 lawyers at the bottom of the sea? I'd call it a start. What's the difference between lawyers and vultures? Vultures don't get frequent-flyer miles.

Introduction

Behind the venom is a feeling that the United States has too many lawyers at work: 896,140 in 1995, to be exact. The American Bar Association, which keeps statistics, says the number of trial lawyers is impossible to estimate. More to the point is that although America has only 5 percent of the world's population, we employ 75 percent of its lawyers.

Yet, despite rising law school tuition, and a shrinking legal job market, this glut continues. By the year 2000, the United States is expected to have 1 million lawyers.

America's so-called litigation explosion raises serious questions. Should McDonald's have been ordered to pay $2.9 million for selling hot coffee that burned an elderly customer when she spilled it onto her lap? Should a transit authority owe $9.3 million to a drunken man who fell onto subway tracks? Are lawyers ruthlessly concocting these cases just to earn huge chunks of the settlements? Such criticism usually centers on personal injury suits, not major criminal or civil rights cases like those in this book.

In fact, frivolous lawsuits have begun to decrease, according to the National Center for State Courts. Jury awards are often adjusted from the bench; the judge in the hot coffee case, for example, reduced the award by 75 percent.

Trials are relatively rare events. Most civil complaints are settled out of court, and indicted felons—as many as nine in ten in New York City—often accept plea bargains in which they plead guilty and are sentenced with no trial.

Men still outnumber women in law as a whole, and especially in the courtroom. Ratios are improving, however. In the 1970s, only about 7 percent of lawyers and judges were women. By 1995, the figure was close to 25 percent.

Furthermore, in America's 176 law schools, currently 40 to 45 percent of the students are female. That's a huge increase jump from the 1870s, when Belva Lockwood fought to be admitted, and even from the 1960s, when Sarah Weddington's class had five women and 115 men.

With each graduating class, the profession becomes more gender-balanced.

Disturbingly, however, a performance gap exists. The Law School Admission Council found that women law students participate less than men do in class, get lower grades, and thus earn fewer perks like law review membership and internships. Women students aren't less intelligent or ambitious; they just seem to have a more difficult time in law school. "Whatever ideals we came in with, get bashed out of us," an anonymous study participant lamented. "Condescending and intimidating" is how another woman described some professors and fellow students.

Blacks, Hispanics, and other minorities of both sexes are gaining a greater presence in the profession. In 1985, only 9 percent of law students were minorities; by 1994 their ranks had doubled. Currently only 4 percent of practicing lawyers are minorities, but the numbers are bound to rise.

Becoming and being a lawyer is rarely easy for anyone. The demands of law school, fierce competition for jobs and clients, and being the butt of insults can take a toll. "I honestly believe that law is a psychologically dangerous profession, [one] that often distances the practitioner and walls him [or her] off from his [or her] own feelings," says Steven A. Ager, M.D., a New Jersey psychiatrist who specializes in treating lawyers.

Indeed, when researchers at Johns Hopkins University measured how often depression occurs among people in 104 different professions, law ranked first. Dr. Ager believes this is because many lawyers—especially litigators—get locked into adversarial roles and can't step back.

The people profiled in these pages love their work. Many claim to have fought each case "as if my own life were at stake." Deep passion for causes and clients is often the most distinguishing factor of a great courtroom lawyer.

This book tells the story behind landmark cases involving rights of Native Americans, the teaching of creationism versus evolution, school desegregation, war crimes, flag burning, spousal murders, rape, and abortion. These issues are still generating headlines—and new cases.

If the intense, high-energy world of trial law attracts you, pursue it. Visit your local courts, which are open to the public. Ask the nearest law school if you can sit in on moot court sessions, and perhaps take part.

The law is a living thing, and the courtroom is the arena where its most compelling dramas are played out.

Belva Lockwood
(1830–1917)

Belva Lockwood was the first woman lawyer admitted to practice before the Supreme Court, the first qualified woman to run for president, and a staunch defender of Civil War veterans and Cherokee Indians.
(Swarthmore College Peace Collection)

People laughed when Belva Lockwood said she wanted to be a lawyer. Go back to teaching school and keeping house for your husband, she was told. People won't trust important legal matters to a woman.

If she had been less courteous, Lockwood could have had the last laugh. Within a few years of completing law school,

> ❦ "Fight, fight, fight everlastingly, not with your claws and fists, but with your wits."

her practice was so busy that she bought a three-wheeled cycle to speed the trip between her office and the courthouse. This was when horse-drawn carriages were the norm, and cycles were so new that the sight of one stopped traffic! Lockwood had the contraption specially designed, with a dashboard to keep her voluminous skirts and petticoats in place.

Belva Lockwood was progressive yet practical. "I am very simple-minded," she once said. "When I wish to do a thing, I know only one way—to keep at it until I get it." Through her persistence she overcame outrageous obstacles. And she had a grand time doing it.

Belva Lockwood was born Belva Ann Bennett on October 24, 1830, near Niagara Falls, in Royalton, New York. Her parents, Lewis and Hannah, were farmers. She had a typical rural childhood: chores, classes in a one-room schoolhouse, roughhousing with a brother and three sisters, and church on Sunday. No one suspected that this "dirty-faced girl," as she called herself, would achieve so much.

However, Belva was "not afraid of snakes or rats or nothing, as active as a boy." She took her Bible study seriously. Awed by Jesus' ability to walk on water, young Belva tried it. When she read that faith could move a mountain, she heaped up some dirt and spent a day staring at it. Finally she attempted a miracle that would matter, praying to bring a neighbor's deceased child back to life.

As an old woman, Lockwood recalled these failed efforts with amusement and respect. They did, after all, hint at the pathblazer who emerged: "I [never] raised the dead," she said, "but I have awakened the living."

When her father wouldn't pay for Belva's high school education, she earned her tuition by teaching summer school. The man who interviewed her wondered only if Belva could stand up to boys who would make trouble. She did, with humor and grit. It was not unlike the way Belva handled some judges and senators who tried to block her progress as a lawyer decades later.

College seemed out of reach, and at the age of 18, Belva married Uriah McNall, a young farmer. He suffered a fatal accident at a sawmill, leaving Belva a twenty-three-year-old widow with a four-year-old child. She later said that when she saw Uriah open his eyes after his accident, it was the first and last time in her life she lost control of her emotions.

To support herself and her daughter, Lura, Belva decided to return to teaching. She was about to accept an offer when she asked how much male teachers with similar experience and responsibilities were paid. Double or more, she learned. It enraged her.

"I kicked to the school trustees," she said. "I went to the wife of the Methodist minister. The answer I got opened my eyes and raised my dander. 'I can't help you; you cannot help yourself; for it is the way of the world.'"

Belva refused the job, asked her parents to care for Lura temporarily, and enrolled at Genesee College (later Syracuse University) in Lima, New York. Three years later she returned with a diploma. For the next eight years, the McNalls remained in upstate New York, where Belva was a teacher and principal at several schools. She achieved equal pay only when she founded her own school in 1863.

The career of Belva McNall, educator, foreshadowed that of Belva Lockwood, lawyer. She had new ideas about learning and equality; she dared to teach her female students physical education and public speaking along with math and botany. Later she wished she had introduced law into the curriculum: "Every lady's daughter [should] be versed in the law, that she may be early schooled to a necessary protection of herself and her children."

In the 1860s the Civil War brought upheaval, new boundaries, and the end of slavery to America. With much debate over the rights of freed slaves, some women began to ask why their rights were no greater than those of children. Married women were considered their husbands' property, and no woman could vote.

Affected by this mood of change, Belva sold her school in 1866 and moved with Lura to Washington, D.C. The city was a dramatic change from small–town life, a "seething pot where I can learn something of the practical workings of the machinery of government and see what the great men and women of the country think and feel."

Giddy with the new possibilities, Belva applied to the foreign service. Rejection for lack of qualifications made her more realistic, and she opened one of the first coeducational private schools in the city. At night she rented classroom space to progressive clubs and attended some of their meetings herself. Her chief cause was suffrage, or voting rights, for women.

In 1868 Belva married Ezekiel Lockwood, a dentist and Baptist minister who had been a Civil War chaplain. He was 65 and she was 38, but they were well–matched in interests and temperament. In 1869 after the birth of their daughter, Jessie, Ezekiel retired from dentistry to run Belva's school. He also became an independent agent handling war veterans' back pay claims against the government.

Since reading the Constitution in college, Belva Lockwood wanted to study law. She put that dream aside while raising Lura, then reconsidered it during Jessie's infancy. Grief striken when Jessie died suddenly of typhoid fever at age 18 months, Lockwood threw herself into her new goal. At the time, few law schools admitted women. As Lockwood's rejection letter from Columbia College explained: "Such admission would . . . distract the attentions of the young men." In 1870 Lockwood and 14 other women entered a new law program at National (later George Washington) University in Washington, D.C. They attended classes apart from the men. Only Lockwood and one other woman finished the two-year course.

Belva Lockwood

The university withheld those two diplomas, because the male students objected to women graduates. Without a diploma and admission to the bar, Lockwood could practice only in police and probate (will-related) courts. In a life filled with challenges, she later called the fight for her diploma "the real fight of my life."

First, Lockwood tried her only alternative, being sponsored by a current member of the bar, and taking a three-day oral exam. She felt she did well, but the examiners refused to report the results. After 16 months of being stonewalled, Lockwood fired off a note to President Ulysses S. Grant. The nation's president was also president of National University, although he had no real function at the school.

> *Sir: You are, or you are not, President of the National University Law School. If you are its President, I desire to say to you that I have passed through the curriculum of study in this school, and am entitled to, and demand, my diploma. If you are not its President, then I ask that you take your name from its papers, and not hold out to the world to be what you are not.*
>
> *Very respectfully,*
> *Belva A. Lockwood*

Her diploma arrived in a week, with no explanation. One colleague welcomed her to the District of Columbia bar with the assurance she would be "treated like a man."

Lockwood's private practice was an immediate success. Her perseverance against social obstacles worked in her clients' favor, as shown by her first case. *Mary Ann Folker v. Frederick Folker.*

The plaintiff sought to divorce her husband (a rare act in the 19th century) on the grounds of his drunkenness, cruelty, and desertion. The judge granted the divorce without fuss, and even ordered the defendant to pay alimony. When Folker said he wouldn't, the judge shrugged.

"The judge told me there was no law to make him pay," Lockwood recalled. This was true; alimony was on the honor system. But plain debt was not. "I showed him I could issue

> ❦ "Let us see what a few earnest, capable women can do."

a *ne exeat* [a warrant against a debtor]. The man was clapped into prison until he agreed to pay the alimony."

In another case, whose name is lost to history, Lockwood turned a woman's second-class status to her advantage. Her client was the wife of a thief. He had given her his gun and ordered her to shoot a police officer who was searching their home for stolen goods. It galled Lockwood that the husband wasn't on trial.

Lockwood argued that because the law commanded a wife to obey her husband, the women had actually obeyed the law by firing the shot. Indeed, the jury found her not guilty. The husband's fate is unknown.

Lockwood's practice was not limited to divorces or women's issues. She handed contracts, wills, and other civil and criminal matters. One unusual case arose, however, that led to her historic entry into the federal courts.

In 1874, Charlotte von Cort hired Lockwood to handle a copyright infringement suit against the United States. Von Cort's late husband had designed and patented a torpedo boat that the U.S. Navy had copied without making proper payment to his heirs. Like any claim against the government, it had to be argued in the specialized U.S. Court of Claims.

Because Lockwood had not yet practiced in a federal court, she needed to apply. The process, usually routine, hit a snag. "Mistress Lockwood, you are a woman," one justice said by way of explanation. "I at once pleaded guilty to the charge," Lockwood later joked. But the justices were not amused, nor swayed by Ezekiel's testimony of support for his wife's efforts. They rejected her application. Court of Claims Chief Justice Charles C. Nott even declared that women shouldn't be practicing law at all, much less in federal courts. If Lockwood wished to try, he suggested, she would have to write a law of her own and get it passed.

Lockwood immediately set to work. She knew the mechanics of legislation; in 1870 she pioneered the first bill to achieve equal pay for equal work for female employees of the civil service, and went on to spearhead many other laws. Eventually the House of Representatives drafted Bill 1077, also known as "Mrs. Lockwood's Bill." It allowed qualified women attorneys to practice in all federal courts, including the Supreme Court.

In the meantime, Lockwood found ways to handle pending cases. All plaintiffs and defendants—female or male—have the right to represent themselves, and Charlotte von Cort did so under Lockwood's instruction. For some other claims, Lockwood did the legwork and turned the courtroom presentations over to male lawyers.

"Mrs. Lockwood's Bill" bounced back and forth, unresolved for almost five years. The Senate told the Supreme Court to make its own rules about admitting women. The Supreme Court wanted the decision to come from the Senate. These were difficult times for Lockwood, who was also caring for her dying husband. Nonetheless, she swore to lobby Congress every year until the bill passed. No one doubted her resolve.

Supreme Court Chief Justice Morrison I. Waite reminded Lockwood that American law derived from English law, which had no history of admitting women to the bar. She reminded him that Queen Elizabeth and other influential women made laws and enforced them. Besides, as she told a convention of suffragists, "It is the glory of each generation to make its own precedents."

The battle was lively, and the newspapers loved it. They often quoted Lockwood, and featured her in editorial cartoons, caricaturing her flowing black skirts—she always chose clothes and shoes that were comfortable—and her look of sharp amusement. When Lockwood hired two female law partners, Marilla Ricker and Lavinia Dundore, the press quickly dubbed them "the three Graces." Like many famous

BELVA LOCKWOOD,
THE EMINENT BARRISTER,
OF WASHINGTON, D. C.,

Who represented the Universal Peace Union at the Paris Exposition, and was their delegate to the International Congress of Peace in that city in 1889, and who was again elected and served as the delegate of the Peace Union to the International Peace Congress in London in 1890—making effective addresses in both congresses, one on "Arbitration" and the other on "Disarmament"—and who is one of the delegates of the Peace Union to the Congress in Rome the present season, is now prepared to favor Churches, Colleges, Teachers' Institutes, and Lecture Committees with any one of the following lectures, viz:

1. **The Paris Exposition and Social Life in Paris and London.**
2. **Is Marriage a Failure? No, Sir!**
3. **Women in the Professions.**
4. **Social and Political Life in Washington.**
5. **Across the American Continent.**
6. **The Tendency of Parties and of Governments.**
7. **The Conservative Force of the College and University with Practical Thoughts on University Extension.**

Lockwood commanded such high fees as a speaker that her lecture agent suggested she give up the courtroom for the podium.
(Swarthmore College Peace Collection)

lawyers to come, Lockwood would be branded a publicity-seeker.

"Mrs. Lockwood's Bill" finally passed in February 1879, thanks to a clever argument by a sympathetic senator. He suggested that the bill's purpose wasn't merely to help women lawyers, but to ensure the right of *all* citizens to hire any lawyer—male or female—they might choose.

On March 3, 1879, Belva Lockwood stood before Chief Justice Waite and became the first woman admitted to practice before the Supreme Court. Within a few days, a similar scene took place before Chief Justice Nott in the U.S. Court of Claims. A year later, Lockwood had the pleasure of returning to the Supreme Court to sponsor Samuel R. Lowery, the first southern black man to be admitted to practice before the Court. She believed the legal profession should be open to all who were qualified, and went out of her way to help women and minority lawyers get a foot in the door.

With the full arena of law now open to her, Lockwood was busier than ever. Her daughter, Lura, was her office manager. At one point Lockwood noted: "For 16 consecutive years I have practiced law, and 13 of them have been passed in court every day," mainly in the U.S. Court of Claims. In that period she estimated having, in addition to a steady stream of general business, "collected about 1,000 pensions and other claims" for clients, more than one a week. The tricycle she used for commuting got a vigorous workout.

The bulk of Lockwood's courtroom work was not glamorous, but it was important. By securing pensions and back pay for war veterans and those of the working class, she improved their lives. At the same time, she paved the way for other women lawyers by supporting their efforts. Even Lockwood's old nemesis, Chief Justice Nott, grudgingly grew to respect her and her female colleagues.

In 1884 and 1888, despite her schedule, Lockwood found time to run for United States president. She was the first qualified woman to do so. (Some history books mistakenly name Victoria Woodhull as the first woman presidential can-

> ❦ "Brains are what Belva is troubled with," wrote a reporter from the *Brooklyn Daily Eagle*.

didate, but Woodhull's candidacy fell apart early and she did not appear on the 1884 ballot. Also, being under the age of 35, Woodhull was ineligible to serve.) Surprisingly, fellow suffragists like Susan B. Anthony turned their backs on Lockwood; they wanted her to work within a major party, as they were trying to do, and not as a candidate of the smaller Equal Rights Party.

Although she made a decent showing in 1884, world peace became her main cause, and she represented the United States at international conventions for 25 years. She also served on the nominating committee of the Nobel Peace Prize.

Like many public figures, Lockwood went on the lecture circuit. In the days before radio and television, audiences flocked to see and hear famous people. Lockwood's repertoire of talks included "Social and Political Life in Washington" and "Is Marriage a Failure? No, Sir!" Her appearances helped increase business for her law firm.

However, it was a professional connection that led Lockwood to her biggest and most significant case—one that affected virtually every Native American rights case since.

Early in her career, Lockwood befriended Jim Taylor, a Native American from North Carolina. They met at the U.S. Court of Claims, where Taylor presented petitions for fellow members of the Eastern and Emigrant Cherokees. In 1891, Taylor convinced his tribe to let Lockwood handle its enormous claim against the U.S. government. Her age—she was 61 then—and her long experience won the trust of the Cherokee tribal elders.

This complicated claim had roots dating back to 1835, when a few Cherokees signed a treaty with the government to exchange the tribe's eastern lands—millions of acres in North Carolina, Georgia, Tennessee, and Alabama—for territory in what would become Oklahoma. The signers, who may have

Belva Lockwood

Oklahoma Territory, 1901. Belva Lockwood was in her 60s when she began traveling to this rough land, not yet a state, to prepare the case that eventually forced the U.S. government to pay $5 million to the Eastern and Emigrant Cherokees.
(48RST-7B81, American West Collection, National Archives)

been bribed, were not tribal leaders or representatives of the majority. The chief of the Cherokee Nation disowned the so-called Treaty of New Echota, as did the Inspector General of the U.S. Army. Nonetheless, the government used it to drive the Cherokees from their ancestral homes.

The forced march of 14,000 Cherokees to Oklahoma in the winter of 1838 is well-documented. Almost one-quarter of the marchers died along the "Trail of Tears." One army man of the time, John G. Burnett, called the relocation "the most brutal order in the history of American warfare."

About a thousand Cherokees, soon to be known as the Eastern Band, stayed behind in the Great Smoky Mountains. Following years of disputes with the Western Cherokees, they

❦ **B**elva Lockwood's reply, at age 80, to a man who asked if she considered herself a "new" or liberated woman:

"As a rule I do not consider myself at all. I am, and always have been, a progressive woman... I do not believe in sex distinction in literature, law, politics, or trade."

signed a treaty in 1891 that freed them to collect their share of the lump sum still due from the 1835 treaty. That was how Lockwood came in.

The federal government agreed that it owed the Eastern Cherokees $1 million. But it also owed an additional $4 million in interest on the 56-year-old debt, which it refused to pay.

To build the case, Lockwood had to take affidavits from thousands of Cherokees, and clear up dozens of smaller, overlapping land claims. She journeyed several times to North Carolina and Oklahoma, covering thousands of dusty miles by train and bumpy horse-drawn wagon. The Cherokees revered her. Still the trial preparation was a long and tedious process, and Lockwood had to interrupt it for a few years when her beloved daughter, Lura, died. Lockwood took on the care of Lura's young son.

Finally, in 1905, the 74-year-old lawyer with the long black skirts and shrewd dark eyes strode once more into the U.S. Court of Claims. Again she faced Chief Justice Nott, the nemesis who had tried to bar her entrance 26 years earlier.

The painstakingly gathered facts of the Cherokee case were in order, and Lockwood's presentation was strong. Judge Nott concluded: "The United States are placed in the position of having broken and evaded the letter and spirit of their agreement." However, the Court granted only partial payment of the interest. Lockwood promptly filed an appeal to the Supreme Court, seeking full reparation.

And so, 13 months later, Lockwood repeated her arguments before the highest court in the land. One justice inquired why the Cherokees expected to be paid interest at all. "Because it was an interest-bearing fund," Lockwood replied. She was given ten minutes for her summation; when she took almost an hour, no one dared to interrupt.

Lockwood's persistence again paid off. The Cherokees won their additional $4 million. Their triumph set a precedent for all future Native American claims.

At 81, Lockwood was far from retired; she reported having "three heavy law cases in hand." At 83, she fell into debt and lost her home. She said an "unscrupulous admirer" had drained away her savings, but in fact she had been sued by the heirs of Jim Taylor, her Cherokee friend and client. Apparently, after studying the papers Taylor left behind, his relatives felt that he had overpaid her—despite a contract that spelled out their terms of compensation. Lockwood's 14 years of work on the Cherokee case netted her $50,000, a mere 1 percent of the final settlement, and she lost the last $9,000 of it in the lawsuit.

This dark incident did not overshadow Lockwood's final years. Colleagues commissioned a formal portrait and presented it to her at a gala dinner. The painting hangs in the National Portrait Gallery. Syracuse University granted her an honorary law degree. At 84, she made the last of her annual voyages abroad, sent this time by the U.S. State Department to promote peace among the warring nations of Europe.

Belva Lockwood died on May 19, 1917. Although her friends and grandson were grateful that she did not live to see her country's entry into World War I, they regretted her never having had the chance to vote, a right not granted American women until passage of the Nineteenth Amendment to the Constitution in 1920.

It is fair to argue that Belva Lockwood achieved more than any woman of her time, and more than most men as well. Why, then, is she virtually unknown? It's a fascinating question to ponder—one that raises issues about Lockwood's life, our times, and a profession that remained largely closed to women for decades after the death of this pioneer.

Chronology

October 24, 1830	Belva Ann Bennett born in Royalton, New York
1848–53	marries Uriah McNall (1848); daughter Lura born (1849); widowed (1853); prepares to enter college
1857	graduates from Genesee College in Lima, New York (later Syracuse University)
1857–65	works as teacher and preceptress (principal) in private schools in upstate New York
1866–67	moves to Washington, D.C.; begins lifelong involvement with women's suffrage and international peace movements
1868–69	marries Ezekiel Lockwood; daughter Jessie born
1870	Jessie dies; Belva begins law studies at National University (later George Washington University)
1872–73	University withholds diplomas of women students; receives diploma after petitioning President Ulysses S. Grant; admitted to Washington, D.C., bar
1873–1914	maintains an active law practice
1879	"Mrs. Lockwood's Bill" passed, granting women the right to argue before the Supreme Court; becomes first woman admitted to practice before Supreme Court and U.S. Court of Claims

1884	becomes first qualified woman to run for U.S. president, as candidate of the Equal Rights Party
1886–1911	represents the U.S. at first and subsequent International Peace Congress conventions
1891–1905	represents Eastern and Emigrant Cherokee Indians in major claims case against the U.S. government; wins partial victory in U.S. Court of Claims
1906	appeals Cherokee case to the Supreme Court; wins full settlement
May 19, 1917	Belva Lockwood dies

Further Reading

"Belva Lockwood, Lawyer, Dies at 85." *The New York Times,* May 20, 1917.

Brown, Drollene P. *Belva Lockwood Wins Her Case.* Niles, Illinois: Albert Whitman & Company, 1987. The best of the Lockwood biographies written for young readers; well-researched and free of invented dialogue.

Davis, Julia. "A Feisty Schoolmarm Made the Lawyers Sit Up and Take Notice." *Smithsonian,* March 1981. A lively magazine article chronicling Lockwood's life and times, with many editorial cartoons and illustrations.

Lockwood, Belva. "My Efforts to Become a Lawyer." *Lippincott's,* February 1888. Reprinted in Julia H. Winner's *Belva A. Lockwood.* Lockport, New York: Niagara County Historical Society, 1969. One of Lockwood's few written works; the source for many of her quotes in this chapter.

Perdue, Theda. *The Cherokee.* New York: Chelsea House Publishers, 1989. For students. Excels at explaining the conflicts between the Cherokees and the U.S. government, but does not specifically discuss the claims case handled by Lockwood.

Stern, Madeleine B., editor. *We the Women: Career Firsts of Nineteenth Century America.* New York: Schulte Publishing Co., 1963. Contains a meticulously researched chapter on Lockwood.

Whitman, Alden. "Lockwood, Belva." In *American Reformers.* New York: H. W. Wilson & Co., 1985. An accurate overview of Lockwood's accomplishments.

Clarence Darrow
(1857-1938)

Clarence Darrow, "attorney for the damned," was a national celebrity. His outspoken style set the pattern for many of today's criminal defense lawyers.
(Cleveland Public Library)

*W*hen Clarence Darrow entered a courtroom, the atmosphere turned electric. This shambling man with his rumpled clothes and sharp tongue made powerful men quake under cross-examination. He saved cold-blooded killers from the hangman's noose and the electric chair, often not on evidence but by the sheer power of his words.

17

Even more so than most criminal defense lawyers, Darrow was full of contradictions. He debated that life was not worth living, yet he passionately fought the death penalty. He defended laborers, yet hated working with his hands. He battled against teaching the biblical theory of creation in public schools, but counted preachers among his close friends.

Darrow saw both sides of every question and could persuade even the most stubborn person to see whichever side he needed seen. He died world-famous and dead broke. Many people believe he was *the* most influential American trial lawyer.

Clarence Seward Darrow was born on April 18, 1857, in Farmdale, Ohio, and grew up in nearby Kinsman. The area was almost entirely farmland, yet Darrow's parents were not farmers. The Darrows differed from their land-loving, God-fearing neighbors in other ways as well.

Clarence's father, Amirus, trained as a minister but lost his faith; he pieced together a living as a carpenter and undertaker. His mother, Emily, supported women's rights. Their house in town, bought cheaply because of its odd octagonal shape, overflowed with books and progressive ideas that influenced their children.

Clarence, the fifth of seven siblings, always commanded attention: "While I was only one [of a large family], I was the chief one." Few people ever called him Clarence. As a child he was known by his middle name, given as a tribute to anti-slavery activist William Henry Seward. As an adult, he answered to Darrow or Dee.

Bored at school, Darrow preferred to fish or play baseball. On Friday nights he tagged along with his brothers and sisters to meetings of the local literary society, a lively forum for lectures and debates. It was the first place, but not the last, where Darrow dazzled audiences as a public speaker.

His mother's death made 15-year-old Clarence feel that he changed "overnight from boy to man." He set off for

Allegheny College in Meadville, Pennsylvania, where his father had studied. A year later he was home, short of tuition and still restless in classrooms.

In one of the paradoxes that would mark Darrow's life, the rebel then became a teacher for three years; a college degree was not required for the job then. The work seemed easier than his other options—carpentry or farming—and gave him time to reflect on what he really wanted to do. Darrow's students liked him, probably because he abolished whippings and gave them long lunch breaks.

Darrow could never fully explain why he gravitated toward the law. One reason was money; another the lure of "a showy profession, one that lets a man enjoy the limelight." Also, in the complicated psychology that links parent and child, he was doing what his father longed to do. In midlife, Amirus Darrow spent a year at the University of Michigan Law School. (Anyone over 18 who had tuition and references of "good moral character" could apply.) At 19, Clarence did the same. One year later he quit law school and took a clerical job with an attorney in Youngstown, Ohio. There Clarence learned enough to pass the oral examination that was the sole requirement for admission to the Ohio Bar.

At age 21, Clarence Darrow became a classic country lawyer near his hometown. Resolving "horse trades, boundary lines, and private quarrels" might seem an unlikely start to a stellar career, but Darrow said it taught him the all-important relationship between human emotions and the law.

In 1880, Darrow married his high school sweetheart, Jessie Ohl. Their only child, Paul, was born two years later. Darrow soon moved the family to Ashtabula, a larger Ohio town. At Jessie's urging, Darrow made half-hearted attempts to buy a house there. Being denied a mortgage on the basis of his low earnings settled the matter; the young lawyer decided that he and his family were moving to Chicago. Like many ambitious lawyers with small-town roots, from Belva Lockwood to Robert Jackson, Darrow craved a bigger city and a wider world. Chicago mesmerized him, he said, because "the crowds surged back and forth as if they knew where they were going and why."

Arriving in Chicago at age 30, Darrow had to start from scratch, competing with a glut of better-educated attorneys. He didn't care, and he sprinted past the competition by introducing himself to John Peter Altgeld, a Superior Court judge and the author of *Our Penal Machinery and Its Victims*. This book, which Darrow greatly admired, put forth the radical idea that crime stemmed from poverty and injustice, instead of character flaws. The influential Altgeld soon became Darrow's lifelong friend and mentor.

With Altgeld's help, Darrow was hired as a Chicago city attorney (called "corporation counsel"). The job paid an astronomical $3,000, ten times his earnings the previous year. It put Darrow into the courtroom, where he learned trial procedure. No one interfered when he took time off to manage Altgeld's successful campaign for governor.

In 1891, Darrow joined the legal staff of the Chicago and Northwestern Railroad. It was an odd match for someone without interest or training in corporate law, but Darrow liked the money. The job gave him time to write—he published his first literary essay in 1893—and handle a few of his own cases.

One such case was that of Eugene Prendergast, a lurid murder defense similar to those that later made Darrow famous. Prendergast, a lawyer, murdered the mayor of Chicago. To spare him from execution under Illinois law, his defense team argued that he was insane. Prendergast contradicted them under oath.

> ❦ "Even civil lawyers know that poverty is the cause of crime, and that is why they don't practice criminal law. There is no money in it."

Sane or not, Prendergast was the first of 50 people charged with first-degree murder whom Clarence Darrow defended in trials or appeals. Many biographies,

Clarence Darrow

including Darrow's obituary in *The New York Times*, state that *no* client of Darrow's was ever executed; they are incorrect. One client was. Despite appeals by Darrow to his friend Governor Altgeld, his client Eugene Prendergast was hanged.

Although he worked in management at the railroad, Darrow admired the growing labor movement. A nationwide rail strike in 1894 forced him to choose sides. When he finally did, his career soared. His defense of union activist Eugene V. Debs against railroad owner George Pullman made Darrow famous.

In an era of powerful railroad barons, Pullman was the mightiest of all. Pullman Company workers lived in Pullman-built towns, rented Pullman-owned homes, and shopped at Pullman-owned stores. Those who tried to live differently, or to unionize, were fired and given bad references. When the economy sagged, George Pullman cut wages by 25 percent. Pullman didn't lower rents or the price of food at his company stores, however. When he refused to meet with his workers to discuss these matters, they staged a strike.

To show solidarity, other groups struck. Chief among them was the broad-based American Railway Union. Their work stoppage affected postal trains, drawing an antistrike injunction from the government. Interference with the delivery of U.S. mail is a federal offense. Union leader Eugene V. Debs was charged with conspiracy against the railroads and the federal government.

Knowing that Darrow was a railroad insider and labor sympathizer, the union sought his help. About the same time, although Chicago was peaceful, the government sent army troops there to ensure order. Outraged, Darrow quit his railroad job, but not until he negotiated a severance agreement to compensate for what the union couldn't afford to pay him.

Kevin Tierney, a Darrow biographer, said the Debs case set up the battle lines for the next quarter-century of labor litigation. It also showcased the techniques that propelled Darrow to fame.

🐦 "We have 7,000 lawyers in Chicago. One thousand could do all the work."

One such technique was toughness. As Tierney put it: "Cross-examination became an instrument of personal cruelty in his hands." In particular, Darrow always targeted an opposing witness or lawyer as his "goat." This was the person, above all, whom he wanted the jury to hate and disbelieve. Darrow's scapegoating was so effective that even the powerful George Pullman tried to avoid being questioned by him.

Another classic Darrow tactic was the appeal to the jury's "higher nature." Whenever possible, he cast the panel of 12 citizens as epic decision makers. His summations were exhortations that drew overflow audiences. Here is what he told jurors in *Debs:* "This is a historic case which will count much for liberty or against liberty. [Accusation of] conspiracy . . . is an effort to punish the crime of thought."

Critics called such summations "Darrow's all-purpose defense," saying that he argued principles rather than facts, and the only guilty party in his eyes was an unjust society. Darrow didn't disagree, as long as his tactics worked.

However, the Pullman case went awry. As a criminal case, it was adjourned when a juror fell ill with no alternate available. The case returned as a civil action that the strikers lost. Darrow helped to appeal it all the way to the Supreme Court, without success.

Darrow's "dragonslayer" style gave him a 20-year career in labor law. The firm of Darrow, Thomas, and Thompson was the first to focus on this specialty. The Pennsylvania-based *United Mine Workers v. U.S. Anthracite Coal Commission* was a typical case. Darrow mounted a crusade against worker exploitation, with bosses as the defendants. The miners he represented worked underground for 12 hours a day, 365 days a year, yet in 1902 their request for shorter hours shocked the nation. As usual, Darrow painted the bigger picture: "An eight-hour day is not a demand to shirk work . . . [it

Whether in a courtroom or a lecture hall, crowds gathered when Darrow took the podium. In his career he defended 50 people charged with first-degree murder and saved 49 of them from execution.
(Cleveland Public Library)

is] what will make the best American citizen." Success in this case, and others like it, led to major reforms in hours, wages, worker's compensation, and similar areas that shaped the American workplace.

Laborers often became extremely violent during union battles, but Darrow brushed off such concerns and persuaded juries to do the same. "I don't care . . . how many brutalities [unions] are guilty of," he once declared. "I know their cause is just."

Darrow always found time for political interests. In 1896, he and Governor Altgeld helped engineer the first presidential nomination of Democratic populist William Jennings Bryan; in that same year, Darrow ran for Congress. Both candidates lost. Darrow later spent a few years working in the Illinois state government, but did little except try to abolish the death penalty. In the state house he was just another representative; in the courtroom he was a star.

While Darrow's career soared, his marriage declined. The more he worked, the more Jessie clung to home. Some biographers have suggested that she was agoraphobic and that Clarence's nonstop activity masked chronic depression. He admitted: "I keep myself occupied so I might forget myself." In 1897 they divorced, a scandalous act. Six years later Darrow married Ruby Hamerstrom, a journalist. At her urging, he soon completed his first novel, a fictionalized childhood memoir called *Farmington*.

In 1911, Darrow began a pivotal, bitter case. He defended John and James McNamara, labor leaders accused of bombing the headquarters of the notoriously anti-union *Los Angeles Times*. The brothers proclaimed their innocence, but Darrow could not support their assertions. In one of America's first plea bargains, he obtained prison sentences rather than execution in exchange for an admission of guilt.

Labor leaders were furious because Darrow had not consulted them about this surprise tactic. In their eyes, he had double-crossed America's union members, who wore buttons proclaiming "The McNamaras Are Innocent," and funded the brothers' defense. Unions would never again call for Clarence Darrow's services. Many laborers felt their split with "that fence-sitter" was long overdue.

Worse, Darrow was brought up on charges of bribing the jury in the McNamara trial. Like many lawyers, he found he worked best "when it seemed as if *my* life depend-

> ❦ "Through brutality and bloodshed and crime has come the progress of the human race."

ed on the result" of the case. Now his professional life truly did. Darrow pleaded innocent, and represented himself. As always, but with extra urgency, he appealed to jurors' sympathies: "My life has not been perfect. It has been human. I ask you to save my liberty and my name."

The panel returned in 34 minutes with a verdict of not guilty. However, Darrow felt defeated. At age 56, he returned to Chicago dishonored and broke.

Whenever his career flagged, Darrow formed a new law firm. He never lacked for willing partners, given his famous name and the business it drew, but his professional partnerships never lasted. Colleagues found him selfish and lacking in business sense.

Darrow's new enterprise was not a distinguished one, serving mainly gangsters. Darrow left most of the work to his partners and went on the well-paid Chautauqua circuit, a traveling talk show. He debated questions like "Does God exist?" and "Is life worth living?" and always took the "no" position. Being on stage restored Darrow's energy. He started writing again, producing articles and a novel about the death penalty and other favorite themes.

All his life Darrow had been against war, but he dropped his pacifism during the conflict that became World War I. He roused support for America's war efforts so well that the government sent him on tour. This brought him new prestige and vitality. At an age when he might have retired, Darrow entered the most powerful phase of his career.

In 1924, a pair of teenage friends named Nathan Leopold, Jr., and Richard Loeb committed what was called "the crime of the century." Their act, and Darrow's remarkable defense of it, would make headlines today. Leopold and Loeb bludgeoned 14-year-old Bobby Franks to death with a chisel, and dumped his naked body in a creek. Then they telephoned his father anonymously, said they had kidnapped Bobby, and demanded $10,000 for his safe return.

The young men planned each step of their "perfect crime" for months. They knew Bobby Franks casually, but had noth-

> ❦ "Everybody is a potential murderer."

ing against him personally. He simply fit their profile of potential targets; he was a rich boy who attended the private school across from Loeb's house in an affluent Chicago neighborhood.

No crime is "perfect." The killers didn't count on their victim's body being found within hours. Or on leaving behind a pair of eyeglasses with unique hinges that would quickly be traced back to them. Or on being unable to scrub away the blood that soaked the seats of the car rented for the crime. Or on not having alibis that matched. By the time they sought the ransom, the police were already closing in.

In the middle of the night after their arrest, the fathers of Leopold and Loeb came to the home of Clarence Darrow and awakened him. They persuaded him to "assist" the attorneys in the Loeb family who were handling the case.

Darrow always claimed that the roots of crime were poverty and lack of opportunity. How could he explain this crime? The killers came from wealthy, accomplished families. At ages 19 and 18, Leopold and Loeb were college graduates; Leopold was in law school. If Darrow could save them from hanging, he could save anyone. Darrow did.

Darrow's first move was to change the defendants' pleas from not guilty to guilty, a tactic that insured sentencing hearings before a judge, rather than trial before a hostile jury. Darrow added insanity pleas, claiming that Leopold and Loeb appeared sane, but in fact lacked all human feeling. He even claimed that Leopold was disposed toward crime because in college he had studied the gloomy works of the German philosopher Friedrich Nietzsche. Ultimately, Darrow argued that the death penalty would solve nothing; imprisonment was more humane.

Darrow managed to keep a lid on certain aspects of the Leopold-Loeb case. Investigators found letters between the young men that implied a homosexual relationship; the body of Bobby Franks suggested sexual mutilation. Discussion on these explosive matters was confined to the judge's private chambers.

Except for the Nietzsche angle, it was a brilliant defense, but its success owed much to luck. The judge in the case, John Caverly, disliked the death penalty as much as Darrow did. Leopold and Loeb got life plus 99 years in prison. Clarence Darrow earned worldwide fame—some said notoriety—as the "attorney for the damned." This case inspired Meyer Levin's 1956 novel, *Compulsion*, which was adapted for the screen.

Darrow kept in touch with "the boys" all his life, even though he had to fight their families for his fee. The Leopold-Loeb defense exhausted him: "I have never gone through so protracted a strain and could never do it again." Darrow's next case, which affirmed his place in history, was, by contrast, a romp.

Many myths have grown up around the 1925 trial of John Scopes, the Tennessee high school teacher who violated state law by teaching Charles Darwin's theory of evolution. The "monkey trial" was part test case, part publicity stunt, since the state did not routinely enforce its anti-evolution law. The key participants had their own agendas.

The American Civil Liberties Union (ACLU), then trying to expand its operations, helped initiate the case, as did the town fathers of Dayton, Tennessee, greedy for the business a national trial would attract. Scopes—who actually taught physics, not biology—agreed to be "arrested" with the guarantee he would be rehired. Scopes assigned Darwin to be read—the state-approved textbook actually covered evolution—but never discussed in class the biblical account of creation or Darwin's contention that the human race descended from apes.

Into this scenario came Darrow, who begged the ACLU to hire him as soon as he learned the prosecuting lawyer was William Jennings Bryan, his former friend. So eager was

*Darrow (left) and arch-rival William Jennings Bryan during a break in the
Scopes Trial. This landmark case, which concerned the teaching of
evolution, was actually contrived by its key players.*
(Cleveland Public Library)

Darrow to confront Bryan that he worked without pay. Bryan
had become everything Darrow hated: he was rural, religious, anti-scientific, a defender of the anti-labor union
South. Bryan was regarded as the best public speaker in
America; Darrow was next, and Darrow desperately wanted
that distinction.

From the start, the trial had the air of a circus. Local people lined up to be interviewed by newspaper and radio
reporters; stuffed monkeys were sold as souvenirs. When
Judge John Raulston began the trial with the customary
prayer, Darrow and co-counsels Arthur Hays and Dudley
Malone leaped up to object. Religion versus secularism!
Some onlookers booed, others cheered, as they would for the

next ten days. Raulston, however, did agree to stop the daily prayer. The proceedings were more a show than a trial. When the crowded courtroom became unbearable in the July heat, Raulston moved the show onto the lawn.

The high point came when Darrow pulled the boldest trick of his career. Having been denied the chance to call pro-Darwin scientists as expert witnesses, he called William Jennings Bryan as an expert witness on the teachings of the Bible. The judge permitted this unorthodox move, but only to assess the value of Bryan's testimony.

It is ironic to note that the showdown between Darrow the atheist and Bryan the fundamentalist Christian was ruled to be inadmissible evidence. Their encounter may not have changed the verdict, but it made history instantly. Darrow poked holes in Bryan's literal beliefs about the Bible as easily as a child bursts soap bubbles. (This cross-examination was well depicted in the play and film *Inherit the Wind*, which was inspired by the Scopes case, but which varies from the facts in many details.)

Darrow: But do you believe [God] made such a fish that it was big enough to swallow Jonah?

Bryan: Yes, sir. Let me add: one miracle is just as easy to believe as another.

Darrow: It is for you.

Bryan: It is for me.

Darrow: Just as hard?

Bryan: It is hard to believe for you, but easy for me. . . . it is just as easy to believe the miracle of Jonah as any other miracle in the Bible.

Darrow: Perfectly easy to believe that Jonah swallowed the whale?

Bryan: If the Bible said so; the Bible doesn't make as extreme statements as evolutionists do.

Darrow: When was the flood?

Bryan: *I would not attempt to fix the date. The date is fixed, as suggested this morning.*

Darrow: *About 4004 B.C.?*

Bryan: *I never made a calculation.*

Darrow: *What do you think?*

Bryan: *I do not think about things I don't think about.*

Darrow: *Do you think about things you do think about?*

Bryan: *Well, sometimes.*

Spectators roared with laughter.

Darrow cemented his case by pleading Scopes guilty, and waiving the defense's right to a summation. Under state law this deprived Bryan of *his* long-planned closing speech, a crushing blow. Scopes was found guilty, but the verdict was reversed on a technicality because the judge set a fine, a token $100, that the jury should have decided.

Bryan died five days later, prompting some to say that Darrow had cross-examined the old Bible thumper into his grave. Anti-evolution laws continued to be ignored, and were ultimately struck down by the Supreme Court in 1968, although the issue resurfaced with force in the 1990s. Darrow's cases were often decades ahead of their time.

The same could be said of his next two trials. In 1925–26, Darrow took up the cause of Ossian Sweet, a black medical doctor who bought a house in a white section of Detroit. Taunted by protesters, Sweet and his family fired guns from inside the house into the crowd on the street. A man was killed. The case was filled with unanswered questions, and ended in a mistrial. In a retrial, Darrow won an acquittal. He managed to convince a skeptical all-white jury that the issue was not murder but self-defense in the face of racism.

Darrow tried to retire, but was forced back to work by the stock market crash of 1929. He lost his life savings, which were invested in his son Paul's utility business. The old performer went on the lecture circuit one more time, just before radio and talking motion pictures eclipsed that form of enter-tainment. While completing his autobiography, Darrow formed one last firm and tried one more big case. He traveled to Hawaii in 1932 to defend U.S. Navy Lieutenant Thomas Massie and three others accused of killing a Hawaiian man who, with others, allegedly had raped Massie's wife. Darrow resolved the tangled affair by winning pardon for the defen-dants in exchange for dismissal of Mrs. Massie's charges of rape against the native Hawaiians she referred to as "half-breeds." If nothing else, Darrow felt, his efforts contributed to racial harmony.

Still in financial need at age 76, Darrow agreed to head the National Recovery Review Board, whose purpose was to determine if some of President Franklin D. Roosevelt's poli-cies encouraged monopolies. Although Darrow was a lifelong Democrat, he scorned Roosevelt's New Deal as government overkill. His committee's critical report said as much.

Heart disease made Darrow an invalid, and took his life at age 80. Silenced only by death, "America's greatest one-man draw," as the show-business newspaper *Variety* called Darrow, still drew crowds at his wake. Family and friends scattered his ashes in Jackson Park in his beloved Chicago.

"I have always yearned for peace but have lived a life of war," Darrow reflected in old age. "I do not know why, except-ing it is the law of my being." He used the law to fight the wars that mattered to him: battles against capital punish-ment and bigotry, battles for unions and free speech and free thought.

Late in life, Clarence Darrow mourned that no young lawyers were following in his footsteps; the fact is that he was always ahead of his time. His spiritual heirs emerged in the 1960s—William Kunstler was one—and they remain a potent force in American law.

Chronology

—————

April 18, 1857	Clarence Seward Darrow born in Farmdale, Ohio
1876	studies at the University of Michigan Law School
1878–79	works as a law apprentice in Youngstown, Ohio; is admitted to the Ohio Bar; opens private practice
1880	marries Jessie Ohl; son, Paul, born 1882
1888	appointed corporation counsel for city of Chicago
1891	joins Chicago and Northwestern Railway Company as senior counsel; continues part-time private practice
1894	defends Eugene V. Debs in railway strike case; begins career as nationally prominent labor lawyer
1903	marries Ruby Hamerstrom; writes first novel, *Farmington,* published 1904
1911	defends McNamara brothers, labor activists, in *Los Angeles Times* bombing case
1912	brought to trial for jury-bribing in McNamara case; defends himself and is found not guilty
1924	defends "thrill killers" Leopold and Loeb in Chicago
1925	leads defense of high school teacher John Scopes, on trial for teaching Darwin's evolution theory, at famed "monkey trial" in Dayton, Tennessee
March 13, 1938	Clarence Darrow dies

Further Reading

Darrow, Clarence. *The Story of My Life.* New York: Grosset & Dunlap, 1932; New York: Charles Scribner's Sons, 1960 (reprint). Out of print, but available at some libraries. Source for many Darrow quotes in this chapter.

Driemen, John E. *Clarence Darrow.* New York: Chelsea House Publishers, 1992. For young readers. Short yet thorough, featuring more than 40 photographs.

Ginger, Ann Fagan. "Watching Darrow Work a Jury." *Criminal Justice Journal*, Winter 1985.

Ginger, Ray. "Clarence Seward Darrow." In *Dictionary of American Biography*, Volume XI, Part II, Supplement 2. New York: Charles Scribner's Sons, 1958. An excellent overview of Darrow's life and times. It corrects key errors and misconceptions found in many other biographical sources.

Lawrence, Jerome, and Robert E. Lee. *Inherit the Wind.* New York: Bantam Books, 1982. This play, which debuted in 1955, is a fictionalized and altered version of the Scopes trial; the film adaptation is available in video.

Tierney, Kevin. *Darrow: A Biography.* New York: Thomas Y. Crowell, 1979. Perhaps the most objective Darrow biography.

John W. Davis
(1873–1955)

*John W. Davis is as well known for his successful career
as a corporate lawyer as for his unsuccessful defense of
segregated schools.*
(Davis Polk & Wardwell)

*J*ohn W. Davis could have chosen a quiet retirement. At age
79, he had argued more cases before the Supreme Court than
any attorney alive, and his elite corporate law firm was thriv-
ing. He might have finished out his days quite comfortably—
attended by his British valet—at his elegant New York apart-

ment, sumptuous Long Island estate, or winter retreat in South Carolina. Even his body, trembling with complications from diabetes, was telling him to slow down.

Why, then, did this ailing lion plunge into *Brown v. Board of Education of Topeka,* the explosive case in which he argued that "separate but equal" schools were good enough for black children? Davis was not a social crusader. He should have known he was likely to lose. His opponents, the National Association for the Advancement of Colored People, and its brilliant lead lawyer, Thurgood Marshall, had spent decades patiently building up to *Brown.*

The very model of a prosperous corporate lawyer, John W. Davis was always a complex man. To understand what made him so successful, and why he took on *Brown,* we must examine his long and extraordinary career.

John William Davis was born on April 13, 1873, in Clarksburg, a West Virginia boomtown. He was the long-awaited, first and only son in a prosperous family of four daughters. Raised as a southern gentleman, Davis retained his gracious manners all his life. No less an authority than King George V of England called him "the most perfect gentleman I have ever met." His style served him and his clients well. Even a critic like Supreme Court Justice Felix Frankfurter, who often clashed with Davis on big issues, called him "an enchanting advocate with great grace, charm, and distinction."

While growing up, Davis felt as comfortable in law offices as most boys do on the baseball field. His father, John James Davis, was a prominent attorney and U.S. congressman who clearly wanted his son to follow in his footsteps. Indeed, John William's life became almost a copy of his father's, though on a broader canvas. At key times he seemed reluctant to exceed John James's achievements. For example, few nominees decline the honor of a seat on the Supreme Court, but John W. Davis did—preferring a private career as his father had.

Davis's mother, Anna Kennedy Davis, was unusually well-educated for her time. A college graduate, she taught her son at home until he was nine. Her favorite texts were the King James Bible and the plays of Shakespeare. The boy absorbed their rhythms and poetry early, and would use them to great advantage in his career. Any traces of perfectionism in John might be traced back to Anna; when he went off to school and brought home an average grade of 92, she chided him for being "lazy as usual."

Davis earned his undergraduate and law degrees at Washington and Lee University in Lexington, Virginia. He briefly taught law there and enjoyed it, but returned to Clarksburg to become his father's law partner in 1895. A few years later, he allowed himself to be drafted into state politics, but the bulk of his time was spent practicing law.

Amid the usual run of business—property disputes, bad debts, and wills—the young Davis got involved in a labor case. He defended "Mother" Mary Jones, a famous union organizer, and Eugene V. Debs, a Socialist leader, on charges of inciting to riot during a coal miner's strike.

This was a rare affiliation for Davis, who made his fortune representing big businesses. It illustrates a principle basic to all lawyers: allegiance to the client. By definition, attorneys are advocates; like debaters, they take sides that may or may not reflect their own beliefs. Soon after defending Jones and Debs, Davis defended a coal company that was evicting a miner's impoverished widow from her company-owned home. How did he reconcile such opposites? In a letter to his new bride, Julia McDonald, Davis tried to explain: "The lawyer spends his life making enemies in other people's causes."

> ❦ "Human rights and rights of property are not different or antagonistic—they are but parts of one great whole."

In 1899, a year after their marriage, the Davises had a healthy baby girl, but the doctor who delivered her had been drunk, and perhaps had not fully sterilized his instruments. Possibly because post-childbirth fever was then common, or because the doctor was a local man, Davis did not sue for malpractice when his wife soon took ill and died. Her namesake, young Julia Davis, grew up with a pony and a fine education when what she really wanted was her adored father's time. As an adult, she reflected with sadness that the law was not only John Davis's work, "but his amusement, his hobby, his life." Davis's oldest friends always believed he never fully got over his first wife's death.

When Julia was ten, Davis began commuting between Clarksburg and Washington, D.C., where he served two terms in the House of Representatives. When she was 13 and in boarding school, he married Ellen Bassell and moved to Washington. The couple had no children, and Ellen died in 1943.

Realizing that he preferred law over politics, Davis gladly left Congress to accept the post of solicitor general—the lawyer who represents the United States in all Supreme Court cases involving the government. This presidential appointment, a plum for courtroom lawyers, would later be held by Robert H. Jackson and Thurgood Marshall, among others.

As solicitor general, Davis fought successfully for the constitutionality of the draft in World War I and unsuccessfully against child labor (although subsequent cases outlawed it). Above all, he learned the highly specialized craft of arguing before America's highest court. In five years as solicitor general, Davis made 73 Supreme Court appearances. Subsequently, in his private career, he would appear there 68 times more. No lawyer since has broken, or is likely to break, this record.

Davis was on a fast track. The government sent him to Bern, Switzerland, to negotiate the release of American prisoners of war, which he successfully concluded. Soon he was appointed U.S. ambassador to Great Britain. A natural diplomat, Davis loved the work. After a few years he was, however, eager to partake of his own country's prosperity. America was *the* place to be during the "Roaring Twenties." There

"Finest-looking body of men I ever saw," said Davis as he took his seat (front row, second from left) in 1926 for his firm's annual photograph. Like most law firms, Davis Polk & Wardwell did not employ many female or minority lawyers until the 1960s.
(Davis Polk & Wardwell)

were big cars to be bought, grand homes to be built, millions of dollars to be made. He settled in New York in 1921, where he had been hired by a prestigious Wall Street law firm, Stetson Jennings & Russell.

When the government offered Davis a seat on the Supreme Court, he declined. He wanted to be in business, not in chambers. "After my ambassadorship, I was busted," Davis noted dryly. "This happens frequently to public servants." In the 1920s his yearly salary on the Supreme Court would have been $15,000, while the annual compensation he received from his firm was about $200,000—the equivalent of $1.5 million a year today.

One event sidetracked Davis. Half-heartedly, he ran for president of the United States in 1924. Davis was such a compromise candidate that he didn't win nomination until the 103rd ballot at the Democratic convention. *The New York Times* noted: "He was a successful Wall Street lawyer and his political advisers' greatest problem was to keep him from looking and sounding like one." There was almost no contest; America was doing so well that Calvin Coolidge, the incumbent, won easily.

Swearing off politics forever, Davis gratefully returned to work. His presidential bid had made him nationally famous, an asset for his law firm. Davis's name was added to the firm's name. Then, as now, Davis Polk & Wardwell (the firm's current name) attracted blue-chip clients. These included the Ford Motor Company, Standard Oil of New Jersey, Eastman Kodak, the Radio Corporation of America (RCA), and—most important of all—J.P. Morgan & Co.

The Morgan family was America's premier financial dynasty. Under J. Pierpont Morgan and his son, J. P., the Morgans ran an investment bank and related businesses that helped transform the United States from a patchwork of family farms into an industrial world power. Railroads, mining operations, steel plants, car manufacturers—the Morgans arranged the financing of the deals that made such interests grow. To some observers, they were the original robber barons. Many others, including Davis, saw them as the very engine of American business. The elder Morgan was so symbolic of wealth, in fact, that the "Mr. Moneybags" image in the board game Monopoly was said to be modeled on him.

In 1929, America's boom went bust; the stock market crashed and the Great Depression began. Unemployment was widespread and hunger was common, yet the captains of industry were untouched. When Franklin D. Roosevelt became president in 1932, one of his key New Deal promises was to "bust the trusts"—the monopolies and alliances among industrialists and financiers. "There will be no one in [my administration] who knows the way to 23 Wall Street,"

> ❦ **D**avis on corporate law as a career: "It's a grand game."

FDR pledged. That was the address of J.P. Morgan & Company, and John Davis knew the way there extremely well; his own office was right next door.

The lines were drawn. The Morgans were among FDR's first targets, named in a federal antitrust suit against their bank and 16 other banks. Davis scoffed at the charges as "monopoly by addition," but he encouraged the Morgans to support moderate reforms. When Congress passed the Glass-Steagall Act, which prohibited banks from underwriting stock offerings, the Morgans did not rebel. They simply formed the new and separate investment firm of Morgan Stanley. In effect their business doubled—and so did Davis Polk's. The law firm prided itself on being among the few employers not to lay off one person during the Depression.

Another of Davis's talents was to lead his firm into new areas, such as corporate taxation. The federal income tax was created in 1913, but into the 1920s some law firms still believed it might be repealed. Since taxes have only increased in size and complexity, a lucrative expertise for early specialists like Davis Polk & Wardwell was created.

Davis's wisdom was useful when the government pursued J.P. Morgan and 20 of his partners for personal income tax evasion. For several years, these men used legal loopholes to avoid paying tax on their own incomes. "Anybody has a right to evade taxes if he can get away with it," Morgan proudly proclaimed. "No citizen has a moral obligation to assist in maintaining the government. If Congress insists on making stupid mistakes and passing foolish tax laws, millionaires should not be condemned if they take advantage of them." Davis advised his clients to play down such attitudes in public, and to cooperate with investigators, which they did.

Like most southerners of his time, Davis was a lifelong Democrat. But he became a vocal critic of the New Deal and its efforts to redistribute wealth. To him, FDR was committing the cardinal sin: using the law to intrude on individual liberties, and to create public policy.

Indeed, in Davis's eyes, many legal issues boiled down to a contest between the individual (or state), and the federal government. This was almost always the crux of the cases he handled *pro bono*—for the good of the people, without fee. This contest drove him, in his old age, to defend segregated schools. Davis's civil libertarian streak, however, had revealed itself decades earlier.

"I feel this case so deeply that it is hard for me to do it justice," Davis said in 1929. What aroused such passion was the plight of Douglas Macintosh, a Canadian-born professor of religion at Yale who was being denied U.S. citizenship. A minister and a pacifist, the 52-year-old Macintosh was being disqualified because he answered "no" to this routine question: "Are you willing, if necessary, to take up arms in defense of this country?"

U.S. v. Macintosh seemed an open-and-shut case of First Amendment rights to freedom of religion and speech, bolstered by legal precedents in favor of conscientious objectors. Davis won the first round, but lost in Supreme Court. By a vote of 5-4, the justices said that the demands of military readiness outweighed an individual's right not to fight. Davis passed the word along in a poignant note:

Dear Dr. Macintosh,
I blush for my country.
      —J. W. D.

For four years in the 1930s, Davis fought with surprising ardor for another "odd man out." Isador Kresel, the in-house counsel for a New York City workingman's bank that had failed, was on trial for perjury (lying under oath). Normally the patrician Davis did not cross paths with immigrant lawyers from the rough-and-tumble Lower East Side of Manhattan. But Davis sprang to the aid of his fellow lawyer, whom he felt was being treated as a public scapegoat for the

> ❦ "My thinking is that the law is underlaid by absolutes or it is not law at all."

bank's failure. This case, which he lost in the courtroom but won on appeal, marked one of Davis's very few appearances before a jury; he hated that part of the case.

For attorneys who love to grandstand, like Clarence Darrow and F. Lee Bailey, the jury is an essential audience. For appellate lawyers like Davis, however, juried trials are circuses. Appellate lawyers vastly prefer the orderly procession of an appeal: reviewing and evaluating what has gone before (for no new testimony or evidence is allowed); writing the brief;

Davis (second from right) on his 80th birthday, not long after his first Supreme Court argument on behalf of school segregation.
Davis's law partners, some of whom are pictured here, were generally unhappy that he took the case.
(Davis Polk & Wardwell)

and making the oral argument before the judge and opposing attorney in a short allotment of time. Of the latter, lawyer Daniel Kornstein has written: "It is an intense 15 or 30 minutes. . . . One must keep the whole case in one's head, and have ready answers for all the weak points."

In fact, Davis virtually wrote the book in this area. His speech, "The Argument of an Appeal," is a legal classic that contains his ten rules for appellate success:

1. Change places, in your imagination of course, with the Court.
2. State first the nature of the case and briefly its prior history.
3. State the facts.
4. State next the applicable rules of law on which you rely.
5. Always "go for the jugular vein."
6. Rejoice when the court asks questions.
7. Read sparingly and only from necessity.
8. Avoid personalities.
9. Know your record from cover to cover.
10. Sit down.

Davis applied these rules to greatest effect in a 1952 case involving President Harry S. Truman. The popular president had ordered the government to seize some steel mills closed by a strike. With the Korean War on, Truman wanted the mills to be ready to produce weapons.

Lower courts ruled that Truman had exceeded his powers. The government appealed the case to the Supreme Court, where Davis represented the steel companies. With rhetorical thunder, he stated the facts and went for the jugular:

Is it or is it not an immutable principle that we have a . . . tripartite system of legislation, execution, and judgment? Is it or is it not an immutable principle that the powers of government are based on a government of laws and are not based on a government of men?

The 6-3 vote against Truman in the steel seizure case is considered Davis's biggest victory. It brought him lasting legal fame. However, in a final bid for history, Davis took on the school desegregation case.

Davis's daughter and his partners gently tried to dissuade him, in the latter case not least because he had accepted the time-consuming case *pro bono*. The old man was adamant, perhaps because an old friend, Jimmy Byrnes, was the person seeking his help. In 1910 they had been congressmen together. Now Byrnes was governor of South Carolina, one of the states fighting to keep its schools segregated. South Carolina's case, with those of three other states and the District of Columbia, had been merged into *Brown v. Board of Education of Topeka.*

We must ask if Davis defended racial separation because he was a bigot. William Harbaugh, his biographer, called him a "moderate" racist. Davis grew up in a segregated society, but he did criticize the white supremacist Ku Klux Klan, and faced their death threats when he ran for president. As solicitor general, he had struck down a law that kept Oklahoma blacks from voting.

It must be remembered that institutionalized racial inequality had unfortunately been the American norm. *Brown* came just a few years after the desegregation of the armed forces, the civil service, and major league baseball. Davis "simply didn't believe that blacks *yet*—and I emphasize yet—were ready to be integrated," Harbaugh said. "He had an evolving view. To be honest, I believe most of the country at the time did."

Mainly, however, Davis realized that *Brown* would be his last big chance to defend what he cared about most: legal precedent and states' rights. Under Governor Byrnes, South Carolina had set aside $75 million to put its public schools for blacks on a par with

> ❦ "The lawyer must steel himself like a surgeon to think only of the subject before him, and not of the pain his knife may cause."

those for whites. The state was obeying the existing law, and Davis firmly believed the federal government should not intervene.

The NAACP's aim in *Brown* was to overturn the "separate but equal" doctrine put forth in the 1896 Supreme Court decision, *Plessy v. Ferguson.* (This strategy is detailed in the profile of Thurgood Marshall.) Davis's aim was to uphold *Plessy.* He told the court:

> *Somewhere, sometime, to every principle comes a moment of repose when it has been so often announced, so confidently relied upon, so long continued, that it passes the limits of judicial discretion and disturbance.*

But "disturbance," not tradition, was what *Brown* was all about. To Davis's own disturbance, the case had to be argued twice, because the Supreme Court asked the NAACP lawyers, in effect, to go back and do more homework. The Court wanted fuller background on the Fourteenth Amendment and its relation to segregation. Davis knew as much as anyone did about that amendment, which calls for equality under the "due process" clause. His father had been a member of the Congress that ratified it. Davis felt sure that nothing in it meant to rule out segregation, and many legal scholars agreed.

In both oral arguments, Davis made a vivid impression. "No one else in the case came near to matching him for bite, eloquence, or wit," said Richard Kluger in his book *Simple Justice: The History of Brown v. The Board of Education.* And Kruger was no fan of Davis; he vilified him as "a gentleman racist" and "the elegant mouthpiece of entrenched capitalism."

Even Davis's chief opponent, Thurgood Marshall, respected him. Marshall knew what made privileged white southerners tick; he had grown up in a world where they made the rules. Marshall's own father, a railroad porter, earned his living by taking orders from men like John Davis. That era was slipping away; did Davis realize it? Listen to Davis's plea in favor of the "separate but equal" system:

Here is equal education, not promised, not prophesied, but present. Shall it be thrown away on some fancied question of racial prestige? . . . I do not challenge [my opponents'] sincerity . . . but I entreat them to remember the age-old motto that the best is often the enemy of the good.

To Marshall and many Americans, equality was far more than a "fancied question of racial prestige." The NAACP unashamedly did want "the best" for black children. Yet the worst Marshall said about Davis publicly, in *Time* magazine in December 1953, was that he was "all wrong about civil rights."

The Supreme Court agreed. In May 1954, their 9-0 decision outlawed segregation. Davis had "marshaled all the facts totally . . . but there was an inevitability about it all," noted Justice Stanley Reed.

Always the gentleman, Davis telephoned Thurgood Marshall to congratulate him; but the defeat pained him. In the last of his 141 appearances before the Supreme Court, John W. Davis came out a loser. Invited to participate in hearings on the enforcement of *Brown*, he refused. Further, he advised governors and lawyers from southern states not to challenge the decision, "We have met the enemy and we are theirs," he wrote bitterly.

Still Davis had one fight left in him. True to his complex nature, it was one that Thurgood Marshall might have applauded. In 1954, when Americans suspected of Communist connections were being blacklisted and interrogated in hearings run by Senator Joseph McCarthy, Davis defended J. Robert Oppenheimer, a government scientist who had been branded a security risk and fired from his job. Oppenheimer, the renowned physicist, had played a key role in helping to develop the atomic bombs that ended World War II.

It took courage to speak out, as Davis did, during the McCarthy era. He had always been an outspoken civil libertarian, in his own way.

Davis died of pneumonia on March 24, 1955. In a warm tribute to him the day after his death, *The New York Times* included only one sentence on *Brown*. It concentrated instead on the scope and depth of Davis's career, praising him as "perhaps the foremost representative of the American bar."

Davis's chief legacy is Davis Polk & Wardwell. It remains one of the world's premier firms, providing legal advice to businesses, but active as well in international and environmental law. Davis Polk still represents the Morgan interests. Lately the law firm has been involved in the privatization of the Chinese national railroad, a capitalist venture that would have warmed Davis's heart.

Would John W. Davis be less pleased at the long shadow cast by his involvement with *Brown*, which, after all, represented only a small portion of his career? Recruiters from rival firms still mention it to lure away the nation's top black law school graduates, for whom competition is fierce. While Davis Polk & Wardwell has hired lawyers from various ethnic groups since the 1920s—and in recent years has made notable efforts to add more minorities to its legal staff—as of 1995 no black lawyer had yet become a partner at the firm.

Chronology

▬▬▬▬▬▬

April 13, 1873	John William Davis born in Clarksburg, West Virginia
1892	receives B.A. degree from Washington and Lee University
1895	receives law degree from Washington and Lee University; joins father's law firm
1898	elected to West Virginia state legislature; serves one term while continuing private law practice
1898	marries Julia McDonald, who dies after childbirth in 1899; daughter, Julia, survives
1910–12	elected twice to House of Representatives; marries Ellen Bassell (1912)
1913–18	serves as U.S. solicitor general
1918–21	serves as U.S. ambassador to Great Britain (official title is ambassador to the Court of St. James)
1921	begins career as Wall Street lawyer at the firm of Stetson Jennings & Russell, which becomes Davis Polk & Wardwell
1922	rejects appointment to the United States Supreme Court
1924	runs for president on Democratic ticket; loses to Calvin Coolidge
1924–55	is made a partner at the law firm he joined in 1921, specializes in Supreme Court appeals
1952–1954	emerges from semiretirement to argue before the Supreme Court on

John W. Davis

the side of school segregation in
*Brown v. Board of Education of
Topeka*

March 24, 1955   John W. Davis dies

Further Reading

Davis, John W. "The Argument of an Appeal." Lecture to the Association of the Bar of the City of New York, October 22, 1940. Reprinted in *ABA Journal*, Volume 26, 1940.

Harbaugh, William H. "John William Davis." In *Dictionary of American Biography*, Supplement 5, 1951–1955. New York: Charles Scribner's Sons, 1977. Succinct overview of Davis's achievements.

Harbaugh, William H. *Lawyer's Lawyer: The Life of John W. Davis*. New York: Oxford University Press, 1973. The only full-length biography of Davis.

"John W. Davis dies at 81; Lost to Coolidge in 1924." *The New York Times,* March 25, 1955.

Kornstein, Daniel. *Thinking Under Fire: Great Courtroom Lawyers and Their Impact on American History.* New York: Dodd, Mead & Company, 1987. Davis is one of ten famous courtroom lawyers profiled in this excellent book written by an attorney and legal historian.

Malkani, Sheila and Michael Walsh, editors. *Insider's Guide to Law Firms* (2nd Edition). Boulder, Colorado: Mobius Press, 1994. Tells what it is like to work at Davis Polk & Wardwell and other major firms. Includes employee statistics by race, gender, salary, and other factors.

Rousmaniere, John. *Called Into Consultation: The History of an American Law Firm: Davis Polk & Wardwell, 1849–1993*. New York: Davis Polk & Wardwell, 1994. Painstakingly researched; contains invaluable insights into Davis and his firm. Privately published.

Robert H. Jackson
(1892–1954)

Robert H. Jackson cross-examined Nazi leaders at the Nürnberg trials after World War II. He also served, not always happily, as a government lawyer and Supreme Court justice.
(Photo by Harris & Ewing, Collection of the Supreme Court of the United States)

*A*re some crimes so evil that they defy justice. Adolf Hitler and the National Socialist (Nazi) Party systematically killed 11 million innocent people, laying whole nations to ruin, in a twisted quest for German world supremacy. Civilization had ample evidence that the Nazis were criminals; were trials needed to prove it? What earthly punishment could make these arrogant torturers suffer even a fraction of what their victims had suffered?

The Nürnberg Trials, at which Hitler's chief henchmen were called to account, sought to answer those questions. The role of representing the United States as prosecutor fell to Robert H. Jackson, who regarded the work as infinitely more important than any he had done, or would do, as a justice of the Supreme Court.

Always a realist, Jackson knew that convicting the Nazis would not end evildoing for all time. He believed, however, the effort must be made. If all great courtroom lawyers are on a mission, Jackson at Nürnberg was on the biggest mission in modern history.

Robert Houghwout Jackson was born on February 13, 1892, in Spring Creek, Pennsylvania, and grew up in Frewsburg, a farm town in western New York. His parents, William and Angelina, ran a small inn and bred work horses. Robert grew up riding horses and never lost his love for it, not even after Model-T cars appeared in his teenage years. During the decades he worked in Washington, D.C., Jackson lived in a rural part of Virginia because it allowed him to ride horses on weekends. He was a tall, broad, restless man who felt confined if he stayed at any desk for long.

As worldly as he became, Jackson clung to his country roots. His childhood landscape, largely pre-industrial, shaped his world view. The same might be said of Belva Lockwood, Clarence Darrow, and John W. Davis. Independent by nature, he grew up among farmers and tradespeople who lived by hard work and personal responsibility. The Nazi creed of a "master race," and the Nazi war criminal's rationale of "just following orders," violated Jackson's deepest values.

Like many other attorneys, Jackson took up public speaking early. He was class orator at Jamestown (New York) High

School, but skipped college to work for his mother's cousin, a local lawyer. Jackson studied at Albany Law School, and, in fact, completed their course in a year. Because the school demanded 24 months of attendance, he never got his law degree. He was among the last of that era of great lawyers who joined the profession through an apprenticeship and exam. A few states still allow this practice. Jackson eventually earned a B.A. by taking night courses at the Chautauqua Institute, not far from Jamestown, where he probably heard Clarence Darrow lecture and debate.

By age 26, Jackson had become the attorney for the small city of Jamestown. Soon he was representing larger clients like the Jamestown Telephone Company and the Jamestown Street Railway. Phone wires and train tracks were becoming as much a part of the American landscape as barns and cowpaths, and the industrial growth was creating an abundance of work for ambitious young lawyers.

Busy as he was, Jackson had ample time for his wife, Irene, and their two children, William and Margaret, as well as for Episcopal church activities, his beloved horses, and his garden. Home life did not come at the expense of billings. In the Great Depression, when people lucky enough to work were thrilled to earn $30 a month, Jackson netted $30,000 in his *worst* year. "No government job I ever held paid as much," he recalled ruefully. Jackson so loved every aspect of being a "country lawyer" that he wrote a nostalgic piece about it decades later for the *American Bar Association Journal* that lawyers still quote.

Yet the up-and-coming Jackson didn't let his own prosperity blind him to the country's economic woes. When the stock market crashed in 1929, three Jamestown banks failed. Jackson helped them regroup by merging, but he saw something going wrong. His hardworking neighbors were losing their farms and their stores. People desperate for jobs could not find them.

In 1931 Jackson campaigned for Franklin D. Roosevelt, the New York Democratic governor running for president under the banner of a "New Deal" for economic recovery. Jackson knew FDR slightly through state Democratic Party politics, and the two men admired each other. He liked the message, later expressed in FDR's inaugural address: "The test of our progress is not whether we add more to the abundance of those who have much; it is whether we provide enough for those who have too little."

The great American director Frank Capra made a movie during the Depression called *Mr. Smith Goes to Washington*. Mr. Smith, played by Jimmy Stewart, is an idealistic hick who stumbles into a Senate seat and triumphs over the corruption around him. When Robert Jackson went to Washington at age 42, he was not *quite* a "Mr. Smith." He came not to hold office but to handle a high-level lawsuit at the request of newly elected president Roosevelt. He was too sophisticated to amuse reporters by making duck calls, as Mr. Smith did. But there are parallels. Ingrained in both men was the belief that small-town residents are as smart as anyone, and that the key to democracy is old-fashioned fairness for all.

A shrewd judge of talent, Roosevelt positioned the country lawyer from Jamestown against one of America's heaviest hitters, financier and former U.S. Treasury secretary Andrew Mellon. Jackson came through. As a lawyer for the Bureau of Internal Revenue, he won a suit that forced Mellon to pay $750,000 in back taxes and penalties. At the same time, government attorneys were investigating other wealthy public figures for tax evasion. Among them was financier J. P. Morgan, who was represented by John W. Davis. By prosecuting these millionaires, FDR was sending a clear Democratic message to the big money interests—and to jobless voters.

Jackson expected to dust off his hands and return to his well-balanced life, but FDR had more work for him. He left Jamestown behind to climb the federal legal ladder: acting as counsel for various government departments; becoming assistant attorney general, solicitor general, and attorney general.

In these roles—especially as solicitor general, who argues cases for the government before the Supreme Court—Jackson mainly defended challenges against FDR's New Deal legislation. He did it well, and is best remembered for his impassioned defense of Social Security, then a new program. The idea of a federal tax on income to help the elderly avoid poverty was a radical notion; skeptics thundered that it would "destroy initiative, discourage thrift, and stifle individual responsibility." Jackson deftly refuted the challenges, and Social Security prevailed, to the point where it has become a sacred part of American life. His arguments have since influenced similar debates over every kind of social program.

By contrast, Jackson had no success defending FDR's controversial plan to expand the Supreme Court beyond its traditional nine members. The idea was that one new justice would be added for each member who reached age 70, to a maximum of 15. Critics said the president was simply trying to "pack" the top court with his cronies. Maybe this is why Jackson received a rather cool reception when FDR appointed him to the Court in 1941.

Although Jackson was a memorable Supreme Court justice, he did not always like the job. Maybe he missed the more active life of the courtroom advocate; certainly he hated the cloistered atmosphere. The day after the Japanese bombed Pearl Harbor and forced the United States to enter World War II, the Court heard arguments about the tax deductibility of player's fees at golf courses. "I sputtered much about hearing such a damned petty question argued all day when the world was in flames," Jackson seethed.

Most Court issues were more vital and relevant. At the height of wartime patriotism, in *Barnette v. West Virginia Board of Education*, Jackson defended the right of Jehovah's Witnesses *not* to salute

> ❦ "[T]he post of] Associate Justice of the Supreme Court is a long way from the farm in Spring Creek."

the flag in public schools, on grounds that it violated their freedoms of speech and religion. This decision was courageous during World War II, when the students—and some of the justices—were taunted as traitors. But Jackson's opinion is still cited by lawyers, most recently in cases concerning the legality of school prayer. These are its most memorable lines:

> *If there is any fixed star in our constitutional constellation, it is that no official, high or petty, can prescribe what shall be orthodox in politics, nationalism, religion, or other matters of opinion or force citizens to confess by word or act their faith therein.*

The year 1945 brought FDR's death, Hitler's suicide and Germany's subsequent surrender, America's use of the atomic bomb on Hiroshima and Nagasaki, and an end to World War II. Allied victors were clamoring for a war crimes trial. The new president, Harry S. Truman, was in full support. He asked Jackson to represent America at what became officially known as the International Military Tribunal.

Jackson was thrilled, and not only because the job involved time off from the Supreme Court. It was his chance to do something for posterity. "I had always loved advocacy and trial work," he said, "and this was about the most important trial that could be imagined."

Before a single Nazi could be called to the stand, the trial format had to be decided; there was no model to follow. Victors throughout history had tried their enemies, but never on an international scale. The legal systems of the participating Allied countries were different. For example, the presumption of innocence ("innocent until proven guilty") is an Anglo-American concept; the opposite is assumed in France. Most European nations, furthermore, do not have trials by jury; there, judges decide all cases.

Jackson traveled to London to hold talks with his Allied colleagues. First, the four countries (the U.S., Britain, France, and the Soviet Union) agreed only that the trials

Nürnberg was a favorite rallying spot for the Nazi Party. Marching ahead of Adolf Hitler during this 1928 parade was the medal-laden Hermann Göring, who faced trial 17 years later in the city's Palace of Justice.
(242-HAP-1928-46, National Archives)

would not be a "kangaroo court," held merely for show. Due process would be followed. Jackson convinced the others to include as few witnesses as possible, mainly for reasons of time; the case would stand or fall chiefly on evidence and courtroom testimony from the 21 Nazis to be tried. (A 22nd had escaped but would be tried *in absentia*; he was later found dead.) Eventually it was decided to hold the trials

> ❦ "We will show [the Nazis] to be the living symbols of racial hatred, of terrorism and violence, and of the arrogance and cruelty of power."

before four judges—one from each Allied nation—and four alternates. There would be no jury, nor any appeal from the sentences. Perhaps most important, defendants would be held individually accountable; crimes could not be blamed on their superiors.

The trial site was Nürnberg, a much-bombed German city chosen because its massive courtrooms and prison were, ironically, undamaged. Not long before, Nazis had marched through its beautiful streets, rallying and chanting "Heil Hitler." Now Nürnberg lay covered in rubble and thousands of dead bodies. The streets echoed with the sound of the Allied clean-up crews and their bulldozers.

Nürnberg's Palace of Justice, the setting for the trials, was a ghostly, castle-like fortress. An attached annex held rows upon rows of very secure jail cells. The Nazi defendants now occupied these dank holes, the same ones where they had imprisoned their enemies.

The two-story courtroom was cavernous, paneled in dark wood that reflected the gloomy glow of bare light bulbs. Each day, teams of lawyers, defendants, translators, journalists, and photographers took their assigned places after being body searched by U.S. Army guards. Armed soldiers lined the entry hall, ready to machine-gun any Nazi who tried to escape. The guards went on special alert during blackouts, for the city's war-damaged electrical lines were not reliable, and sometimes the windowless courtroom was plunged without warning into utter darkness.

Historians give varying grades to the Nürnberg Trials and Robert Jackson's role in them, but all agree that his opening statement is among the most brilliant trial addresses ever. "My spine throbbed," said William L. Shirer, author of the definitive history of Hitler and the Nazis, *The Rise and Fall of the Third Reich,* who sat in the journalist's dock that morning of November 21, 1945. Jackson began:

May It Please Your Honors:

The privilege of opening the first trial in history for crimes against the peace of the world imposes a grave responsibility. The wrongs which we seek to condemn and punish have been so calculated, so malignant and so devastating, that civilization cannot tolerate their being ignored because it cannot survive their being repeated. . . .

In the prisoners' dock sit twenty-odd broken men. . . . It is hard now to perceive in these miserable men as captives the power by which as Nazi leaders they once dominated much of the world and terrified most of it. Merely as individuals, their fate is of little consequence.

What makes this inquest significant is that these prisoners represent sinister influences that will lurk in the world long after their bodies have turned to dust.

Much of Jackson's four-hour-long address centered on the legal framework. Each defendant would be found guilty or innocent on four charges: Count 1, The Common Plan, or Nazi Conspiracy; Count 2, Crimes Against Peace; Count 3, War Crimes; and Count 4, Crimes Against Humanity. Every Nazi pleaded "not guilty." Jackson ended his opening address by exhorting the judges:

Civilization asks whether law is so laggard as to be utterly help-less to deal with crimes of this magnitude. . . . It does not expect that you can make war impossible. It does expect that your judicial action will put the forces of International Law . . . on the side of peace.

After this lofty and inspiring start, the gritty courtroom work began. It went on for almost ten months. Repetition is unavoidable in trials with numerous defendants. With 21 defendants, each cross-examined in turn by four different prosecutors in four different languages, the Nürnberg hearings sometimes seemed to crawl. The murmur of translators

Claiming eyestrain, Hermann Göring often wore sunglasses in court. Here he waited under guard with 5 of the 20 other high-ranking Nazis on trial. Front: Göring, Rudolf Hess, Joachim von Ribbentrop. Back: Karl Dönitz, Erich Raeder (behind envelope), and Baldur von Schirach.
(238-NT-665, National Archives)

speaking softly into their microphones became a steady backdrop. It was an equally familiar sight to see listeners adjusting their earphones. Sometimes one of the English-to-German translators would mangle a phrase, and the solemnity would be shattered by hoots of laughter from the Nazis and their defense lawyers.

At other times, the proceedings cut to the bone and needed no translation. Even jaded spectators were left gasping when prosecutors presented lampshades made from the skin of slaughtered Jews; projected photos of the mountains of gold fillings systematically extracted from the mouths of the dead; or drew out calm testimony from the Nazis about their torturous medical experiments on twins, homosexuals, and anyone they chose as human subjects—even "good" German citizens with disabilities. The Nazis, for the most part, responded with boredom or annoyance.

Until Robert Jackson introduced them into evidence, no mass audience except Nazis had seen the films that Hitler had made at the concentration camps. Hitler's cameramen had filmed the horrors precisely, in rigorous detail that bespoke great pride. Anyone who has seen the classic Holocaust documentary films *Night and Fog* or *Shoah* can testify to the gruesome effect. Many historians believe that visual evidence alone sealed the case against the Nazis. As the trial went on, physical strains took their toll. Participants lived in spare, army-furnished quarters and ate army food. In World War II parlance, they did not mind "doing their bit," but the devastated city offered no respite. Testiness began to show between Jackson and some of his American colleagues. Jackson was unusually high-strung, and U.S. Judge Francis Biddle and a few others began to see him as high-handed. They delivered a subtle comeuppance during Jackson's cross-examination of Hermann Göring. This would be the most important face-off at Nürnberg, and despite Jackson's strong experience as a prosecutor, it was largely a disaster.

Göring was second only to Hitler in planning and carrying out the Führer's deadly "final solution." Jackson called him "half militarist and half gangster" who "stuck a pudgy finger in every pie." A lover of rich food and a morphine addict, Göring weighed so much when brought to Nürnberg that he had to enter the prison elevators sideways. Drug withdrawal added to his viciousness. He would sometimes laugh and comment during the hearings as if they were a play staged for his amusement. While being cross-examined, he took Robert H. Jackson on a verbal ride—the kind that any judge would normally have nipped in the bud as irrelevant and inflammatory. At the behest of U.S. Judge Biddle, apparently to teach Jackson a lesson, the judges did not intervene.

Jackson: Now, was this leadership principle [dictatorship by Hitler] supported and adopted by you in Germany because you believed that no people is capable of self-government. . . . ?

Göring [as simultaneously translated]: I didn't quite understand the question, but perhaps I could answer it as follows: The Führer's principle proved to be necessary because the conditions previous to his leadership had brought Germany to the verge of ruin. I might in this case remind you that your own President Roosevelt, so far as I can recall—I don't want to quote it verbatim—said that democracy had produced men who were too weak to give their people work and bread. To correct this it would be best for the people to abolish democracy. There is much truth in that statement.

Göring rambled a while longer. After another few rounds, unchecked by the judge, Jackson's mounting impatience showed:

Jackson: By the time of January 1945 you also knew that you were unable to defend the German cities against the air attacks of the Allies, did you not?

Göring: The defense of German cities against Allied bomb attacks, hmm—I will try to give you a picture of the possibility.

Jackson: Can you not answer my question? Time may not mean quite as much to you as it does to the rest of us. Can you not answer yes or no?

Göring went on acting like a bratty child who bedevils one parent when he sees the other will not step in. Jackson and Judge Biddle soon had words privately. Jackson's subsequent cross-examinations of other Nazi criminals, including Albert Speer, Hitler's Minister of Armaments, and Reichsbank director Ajalmar Schacht, went somewhat more smoothly.

The trials ended in September 1946. Jackson's closing statement climaxed in a poetically impassioned plea: "If you say of these men that they were not guilty, it would be as true to say there has been no war, there are no slain, there has been no crime."

Two days later, the four judges read the sentences: death by hanging for 12 defendants, life in prison for four others, shorter sentences for three, and freedom for three. The hangings took place the next day, after midnight.

Soldiers built the gallows so hastily that the platform beneath the hanged men did not drop as it should have. Thus, instead of dying rapidly, they twisted on their nooses for as long as 20 minutes. "Heil Hitler!" one gasped from under his hood. None expressed remorse. Their corpses were burned in the ovens of human death at the Dachau concentration camp, relit for the occasion, and their ashes scattered in the Isar River.

Göring, one of those sentenced to death, cheated the hangman. He committed suicide, as had his beloved Hitler, by swallowing cyanide. Some say the capsule was smuggled to Göring in his cell; others believe the sly man had had it all along, inserting and reinserting the glass capsule in his anus, so far up as to escape routine examinations by military doctors.

Jackson did not witness the hangings. He was already on his way back to Washington and his seat on the Supreme Court. A second tribunal was held later for a group of lower-ranking Nazis; Jackson did not participate in it. President Truman awarded him the Medal of Merit in honor of his work at Nürnberg, yet privately some of his fellow justices expressed resentment at his absence. In photos from the time, Jackson looks extremely weary.

The experience of Nürnberg affected at least one of Jackson's judicial decisions. An ardent champion of First Amendment rights, he dissented in two cases that protected anti-Semitic speech and religious insults. "[To] blanket hateful and hate-stirring attacks on races and faiths under the protection of freedom of speech," he wrote, "may . . . belittle great principles of liberty."

In March 1954, Jackson had a heart attack. Still recuperating

> ✿ "Something does happen to a [lawyer] when he puts on a judicial robe, and it ought to. The change is very great . . . deciding other people's controversies, instead of waging them."

two months later, he insisted on appearing at Court for the announcement of the *Brown v. Board of Education of Topeka* decision, the landmark case that ended racial segregation in public schools. The unanimous decision was a stunning victory for Thurgood Marshall, and an equally stunning defeat for John W. Davis.

Ignoring his doctor's orders to retire, Jackson reported as usual on the first Monday in October for the start of the 1954–55 Supreme Court session. Within a week, on his way to work, another heart attack took his life. He was 62.

Debates over the worth of the Nürnberg Trials went on for years. The trials glossed over war crimes by Allied forces, especially those of Russian leader Josef Stalin. Some scholars question the legitimacy of the trials, under a principle known as *ex post facto* ("after the fact"). They contend that the Nazis were accused of actions that were *not* considered crimes in Hitler's Germany, that they were tried unfairly *ex post facto*. Opinions like this, offered in the wake of 11 million deaths, do not win friends for legal scholars. Certainly Robert H. Jackson rejected them. The very reason for Nürnberg, he said, was to create international laws that would supersede the evil laws of another Hitler. The trials also introduced the concept of international human rights.

People question the value of the Nürnberg Trials as a deterrent. Jackson might have done the same. Atrocities have continued in a dishonor roll of wars and violent outbreaks: Korea in the 1950s, Vietnam in the 1960s and 1970s, Afghanistan and Nicaragua in the 1980s, Serbia and Bosnia in the 1990s. This book's profile of F. Lee Bailey depicts a key war-related trial, that of U.S. Army Captain Ernest Medina, who was charged during the Vietnam War with leading a massacre on the village of My Lai.

Like many trials, war tribunals seem to do too little, too late. "But if we await perfect justice, none will ever be meted out," argues Morris B. Abram, chairman of the international organization United Nations Watch. "What would we want Allied powers in World War II or the United Nations today to do with captured monsters? Shot them on the spot? Turn them loose? Or try them by set rules in an open court?"

In tackling such questions, Robert H. Jackson helped create the rules and precedents by which war criminals are still tried. These are lasting achievements, especially for someone who wanted to be only a simple country lawyer.

Chronology

February 13, 1892	Robert Houghwout Jackson born in Spring Creek, Pennsylvania; grows up in Frewsburg and Jamestown, New York
1910	apprentices in Jamestown law office; attends Albany Law School for one year
1913	admitted to the New York Bar; opens private practice
1916	earns B.A. at Chautauqua Institute; marries Irene Gerhardt
1918–34	becomes city attorney (Corporation Counsel) for Jamestown and general counsel for several Jamestown businesses; is active in state Democratic Party; has a son and a daughter
1934	becomes general counsel for the Bureau of Internal Revenue in Washington, D.C.
1938	appointed U.S. solicitor general by President Franklin D. Roosevelt
1940	appointed U.S. attorney general
1941–54	serves as associate justice, U.S. Supreme Court
1945–46	takes temporary leave from the Supreme Court to act as chief of counsel and prosecutor for the United States at the International Military Tribunal at Nürnberg, Germany
October 9, 1954	Robert H. Jackson dies

Further Reading and Viewing

Aymar, Brandt and Edward Sagarin. *A Pictorial History of the World's Great Trials.* New York: Bonanza Books, 1985. Has a good summary and numerous photos of the Nürnberg Trials.

Berenbaum, Michael. *The World Must Know: A History of the Holocaust As Told in the U.S. Holocaust Memorial Museum.* Boston: Little, Brown & Co., 1993. Stark photographs and words testify to the devastation wrought by the Nazis.

Gerhart, Eugene. *America's Advocate: Robert H. Jackson.* Indianapolis: Bobbs–Merrill, 1958. The only full-scale Jackson biography. Out of print but available at some libraries.

Kelly, Alfred H. "Robert Houghwout Jackson." In *Dictionary of American Biography,* Supplement 5. New York: Charles Scribner's Sons, 1977. Overview of Jackson's achievements.

Jackson, Robert H. *The Nuremberg Case.* New York: Cooper Square Publishers, 1971. A reprint of Jackson's original 1947 report to President Harry S. Truman on the Nürnberg proceedings. Contains the full text of Jackson's opening and closing statements, plus excerpts from four cross-examinations, including that of Göring.

Kurland, Philip B. "Robert H. Jackson." In *Justices of the Supreme Court, 1789–1969: Their Lives and Major Opinions,* edited by Leon Friedman and Fred L. Israel. New York: Chelsea House Publishers, 1969. An excellent short biography spiced with many good quotes from Jackson, taken from interviews he taped for the Oral History Project of Columbia University.

Mann, Abby. *Judgment at Nuremberg.* This fictional movie is based on the second round of Nürnberg trials, in which Robert Jackson did not participate. However, it gives a good feeling for the trials' atmosphere. Available on video.

Thurgood Marshall
(1908–1993)

Thurgood Marshall, lawyer and Supreme Court justice, helped transform the United States from a country of racial segregation to one of equal rights.
(Photo by Hessler Studios, Collection of the Supreme Court of the United States)

A teenager sits restlessly in a classroom on a hot day. He is black. So is every other student in the school, which by state law is for blacks only. Next door is a police station. Through the open windows, the teenager hears officers beating a man until he confesses to a crime. The police are white men; by city law, no blacks or women can serve on the police force.

The suspect is a black man. This scenario is often repeated, but no one protests. The suspect will not be advised of any rights, nor will he have access to a lawyer unless he can afford one. It is simply "the way things are."

Thirty years later, the teenager is a famous lawyer. Arguing before the Supreme Court, he has won the landmark case that will allow children of all races to be schooled together. Thirteen years after that, he will become the first African-American Supreme Court justice.

Throughout his life Thurgood Marshall was restless. He used his energy to crusade for equal treatment under the law for all Americans, especially the poor and less powerful. Always a realist, he knew the job would never end.

Thoroughgood Marshall was born on July 2, 1908, in Baltimore, Maryland. His great-grandfather was a slave who rebelled so furiously that his master set him free. Marshall's parents worked their way into the black middle class, yet their careers reflected the racial division of the old South. Norma Marshall taught in a public school for blacks only, under a white superintendent. William Marshall worked as a waiter on trains, and as a steward at an all-white yacht club. The Marshalls were homeowners and taxpayers, yet because of their race they could not legally enter Baltimore's department stores or public bathrooms.

For Thoroughgood—who began spelling his name "Thurgood" almost as soon as he could write—segregation was a fact of life. "I was taught to go along with it, not to fight it unless you could win it," he said. There was one major exception. "If anyone ever calls you a nigger, you not only got my permission to fight him—you got my *orders* to fight him," William Marshall told Thurgood and his older brother.

> ❦ "My father turned me into a lawyer without ever telling me what he wanted me to be. He taught me how to argue, challenged my logic on every point, even if we were discussing the weather."

The good-natured Thurgood didn't have to fight much. Supported by a close-knit family and neighborhood, he rarely felt uneasy because of his race. He naturally kept bullies at bay, being physically big, and fearless by nature.

In school, where his grades were just average, Marshall was a self–proclaimed "hell-raiser." His teachers had a novel punishment; they made unruly students read the U.S. Constitution. By graduation, Marshall knew it by heart.

At the all-male Lincoln University in Pennsylvania, known then as "the Negro Princeton," Marshall followed his mother's wishes and took pre-dentistry courses. Still a middling student, he was expelled in sophomore year for fraternity pranks. Marrying Vivian "Buster" Burey changed him: "I got the horsing around out of my system."

Returning to Lincoln as a junior, Marshall took more interest in his racial identity. Two years earlier, he had voted with the majority of students to keep the faculty all-white. Now his classmate the future poet Langston Hughes was able to convince Marshall otherwise. Such thinking, said Hughes, perpetuated a "belief in our own inferiority." The faculty soon was integrated, and Marshall changed his major to humanities and pre-law. He and his friends also desegregated the local movie theater. "I guess that's what started the whole thing in my life," he recalled.

The University of Maryland School of Law was Marshall's first choice among graduate schools, but it did not admit blacks. He attended all-black Howard University Law School in Washington, D.C. There he lost 30 pounds from sheer hard work the first year. But at Howard Marshall also found a mentor who shaped his life. Charles Hamilton Houston, the school's vice dean, was active in the National Association for the Advancement of Colored People (NAACP). Houston taught black lawyers to be "social engineers." His master plan was to chip away at segregation laws on the basis that they violated the Constitution, which promises basic freedoms to all Americans. Throughout Marshall's life, he would credit Houston as his greatest influence.

Thurgood Marshall

After graduating first in his class at Howard, Marshall opened an office in Baltimore. With the economy at a near-standstill during the Great Depression, business was slow. To gain experience, Marshall volunteered his services to the local NAACP chapter.

There, in 1935, Marshall won his first landmark civil rights case. Still rankled that Maryland's state-funded law school could exclude blacks, Marshall urged a qualified black student named Donald Murray to apply there. When Murray was rejected, Marshall and Houston took the school to court. They didn't expect to win, but wanted to set the legal process in motion. If necessary Marshall was ready to appeal the case all the way to the Supreme Court.

Marshall's key argument summed up the NAACP strategy: "What is at stake here is more than the rights of my client; it is the moral commitment stated in our country's creed." The state judge ruled in Murray's favor, to Marshall's surprise and lifelong pleasure. The University of Maryland School of Law not only desegregated, but eventually named its library for Thurgood Marshall.

After this victory, Marshall went to work part-time at the NAACP's headquarters in New York City. Commuting by train from Baltimore ate into his annual pay of $2,600. Promoted to Charles Houston's job as director-counsel in 1938, Marshall moved north. He and his wife settled on prestigious Sugar Hill in Harlem, where their neighbors included boxer Joe Louis and jazz great Duke Ellington.

Marshall spent little time at home. He traveled 50,000 miles a year for the NAACP, becoming head of its Legal Defense and Educational Fund. The *Encyclopedia of American Biography* called him "the field general for lawyers in the civil rights movement." His fame spread nationally.

Marshall trained a network of attorneys and supporters. Some wanted to retain the "separate but equal" approach and fight only for "equal" resources for blacks, but Marshall insisted that the battle was against segregation itself. He taught his troops what Houston had taught him: "The secret was hard work and digging out the facts and the law." That was Marshall's lifelong creed, from small-town courtrooms to the Supreme Court. Sometimes he suffered racial slurs; the only time he ignored his father's instructions to fight back was in court. When he "did take a little," as he noted, it was to gain a lot. A friend once explained: "Thurgood never wanted to win a battle if it would lose him the war" for racial equality.

Everything about the NAACP's approach was methodical. They pressed cases at the town or county level, often losing, but always appealing to higher courts at the state or federal level. This strategy was repeated in the 1960s by civil rights lawyers such as William Kunstler. There were many appeals. In 25 years with the NAACP, Marshall brought 32 cases to the Supreme Court. He won 29 of them.

Doing the groundwork was dangerous, sometimes even life-threatening. Throughout his life, Marshall told stories of his traveling days. Often, when he arrived in town, word would spread that strong black men were needed to "sit up with a sick friend." Their real job was to guard Marshall while he slept, against attacks by the Ku Klux Klan.

Once, leaving a Tennessee town where he had just won a case, Marshall was arrested on a false charge of drunken driving. He was ordered to take a sobriety "test" that consisted of breathing in the face of the local judge. At 6 feet 2 inches tall, weighing about 230 pounds, Marshall towered over the elderly man. "I blew so hard he rocked," he later laughed. "I turned around and the police were gone."

Eventually the legal triumphs outweighed the threats. Throughout the 1930s and 1940s, Marshall and the NAACP won $3 million in retroactive equal pay for southern black teachers. In 1944 they helped secure what *Black Enterprise* magazine called "the purest form of black power: the right to vote" in key primary elections. In 1948—the same year Jackie Robinson broke the ban against blacks in major league baseball—a Supreme Court victory found unconstitutional laws that had kept blacks from buying houses in many areas.

Although by 1950 the U.S. Congress still could not pass an anti-lynching law, that year the Supreme Court handed down two key rulings. The Court barred racial discrimination at the University of Texas Law School and at Oklahoma State graduate schools. These victories proved Houston's belief that the best way to start was with black college graduates who, in the eyes of white judges, had "proven" themselves.

> ❦ "He has moved many a judge to search his conscience and come up with decisions he probably did not know he had in him."— African-American poet Langston Hughes on his college classmate and friend, Thurgood Marshall.

With those cases as precedents, segregation began to disappear from professional schools all over the South. Removing racial barriers from schools at all levels would now be a matter of additional cases, hard work, and time.

In 1954, with the Supreme court case *Brown v. Board of Education of Topeka,* the time came. It was the end of segregated public schools that had been legal in 21 states.

The landmark case began four years earlier in Topeka, Kansas. The plaintiff, Oliver Brown, was a welder, not a civil rights activist. His daughter, Linda, had to walk a mile each way through dangerous rail yards to reach the public grade school for blacks. Simply for safety, Brown wanted to enroll his daughter in another school much closer to their home. That school was for whites only, and its principal turned Linda away.

Brown's solid case was what the local NAACP had been waiting for. Other black parents joined the lawsuit, filed in 1951 against the state of Kansas. They lost, but NAACP lawyers immediately appealed. Special rules allowed them to skip the federal appeals level and move directly to the Supreme Court.

The Court held the first hearings on *Brown* in 1952, putting the case on hold for a year, a maddening yet hopeful delay. The court often asks for more time and second argu-

September 8, 1954: One semester after the Brown *decision, this classroom in Fort Myer, Virginia, became one of the first in the South to desegregate.*
(Photographs and Prints Division, Schomburg Center for Research in Black Culture, The New York Public Library, Astor, Lenox and Tilden Foundations)

ments in landmark cases; Sarah Weddington faced a similar situation in *Roe v. Wade*, which legalized abortion.

The Court's justices gave Marshall and John W. Davis a clear direction: focus on the Fourteenth Amendment, which ensures equal protection under the law. If segregated school systems clearly violated that amendment, that might convince them to overturn the "separate but equal" racial doctrine laid down by the Supreme Court in *Plessy v. Ferguson* in 1896. When arguing for desegregation Marshall also cited the Fifth Amendment, which ensures due process of law to all citizens.

Teams of lawyers and aides plunged into the fine points of the amendments and *Plessy.* They also gathered sociological and psychological data—then a bold new tactic—to show that segregated schools harmed all races as well as society. The profile in this book of John W. Davis outlines the approach of the pro-segregation side.

Marshall's performance was brilliant. He knew his way around the Court; he knew when to be technical and when to speak plainly. When Justice Felix Frankfurter asked him to define "equal," Marshall said calmly: "Equal means getting the same thing, at the same time, and in the same place."

On May 17, 1954, the Supreme Court struck down school segregation as unconstitutional. The vote was unanimous. "Separate educational facilities are inherently unequal," the decision said.

Brown did not quickly bring a new world of racial equality. Governors and mayors in many southern states made violent last stands against desegregation, often personally barring blacks at school doors. In 1957, at Central High School in Little Rock, Arkansas, President Eisenhower had to send in the National Guard to keep order.

Marshall took a memorable break from the school crusade. In 1951 he went to Asia to investigate reports that many black soldiers fighting in the Korean War were being jailed by the U.S. Army on false charges. Their trials "were what was known as 'drum head' court-martials, which means they were held late at night out of anybody's knowing. And automatic guilt" was always the verdict, Marshall recalled. He had all of the sentences overruled or reduced.

The mid-1950s also brought personal upheavals. Buster had terminal cancer, but kept the diagnosis from her husband until *Brown* was decided. Marshall nursed her at home until her death in February 1955. "She would have done the same thing for me," he said; they had been married 25 years.

After six months—the customary period of mourning among his family and friends—Marshall began dating Cecilia Suyat, an NAACP secretary. They wed in December 1955, and had two sons. Both sons followed their father into public service: Thurgood, Jr., as a lawyer and government advisor;

> 🐝 "**O**ur Constitution is the best of all, with a few exceptions like Kenya's, where I drew the whole schedule of rights."

John William as a Virginia state police officer.

The NAACP continued to enforce the *Brown* decision case by case, and Marshall remained in the forefront of the struggle. In surveys among black Americans, he was equal to Dr. Martin Luther King as the country's principal black leader.

The quest for black equality spread worldwide, with many newly independent African nations seeking guidance from American civil rights leaders. Marshall went to Kenya in 1960 to write that country's constitution and bill of rights. He also advised Nnamdi Azikiwe, president of Nigeria and a fellow graduate of Lincoln University.

As the Black Power movement grew in America, Marshall and the NAACP began to be scorned by blacks who preferred separatism to integration. Black nationalists dismissed him, Marshall said, as a "half-white son of a b———." Marshall had some Caucasian ancestry, but he was not half-white.

A meeting with Malcolm X, the famed speaker for the Nation of Islam, turned into a shouting match. "I still see no reason to say Malcolm X is a great person," Marshall insisted in 1992. "What did he ever do?" Marshall saw little value in violence: "The one thing you get out of race riots is that no guilty person ever gets hurt. The innocent people get hurt."

From time to time, high-paying law firms tried to lure Marshall from the NAACP. The money was tempting, and Marshall was weary of the travel that his civil rights work demanded, but he held out. Then in 1961 President John F. Kennedy nominated him as a judge for the U.S. Court of Appeals, in New York City. In vain, four southern senators tried for a year to block Marshall's appointment.

Marshall's only qualm was that people might think he was abandoning his cause, but his judgeship gave him a wider arena. In various cases he opposed the use of wiretapping to gain evidence, ruled against loyalty oaths for New York teachers, and limited the power of immigration authorities to deport non–U.S. citizens.

Federal judgeships are lifetime jobs, but Marshall stepped down—and took a pay cut—in 1965, when President Lyndon B. Johnson chose him as U.S. solicitor general. His predecessors in his prominent job included John W. Davis and Robert H. Jackson. He was confirmed immediately, unlike four years earlier. The high-ranking post put Marshall before the U.S. Supreme Court again, now as the government's chief advocate. He won 14 of 19 cases, most notably helping to remove the last legal obstacles like literacy tests and poll taxes that kept blacks from voting.

On October 2, 1967, Marshall assumed the job President Johnson may have had in mind for him all along: Supreme Court justice. He was the first African-American on the Court. Johnson called his nomination "the right thing to do, the right time to do it, the right man and the right place."

Massive changes in society, brought about in part by the civil rights movement, ignited racial tensions in the late 1960s. Riots erupted in Detroit, Michigan, Newark, New Jersey, and other cities, as some black citizens protested that the movement had not delivered on its promises. Many Americans hailed Marshall's appointment to the nation's highest court, citing it as proof that the system was working. Others pointed out that few attorneys of any race were so qualified to serve there. But the new justice also had his detractors. For example, conservative newspaper columnist Joseph Kraft saw Marshall as a token who embodied "the outmoded principle of ethnic representation" and would not "bring to the Court penetrating analysis or distinction of mind." Ironically, critics used similar arguments 24 years later against Marshall's successor, conservative Clarence Thomas, who became the high court's second black justice.

On the court, Marshall spoke out forcefully for civil rights and individual liberties. His friend and colleague Justice William Brennan said Marshall's power came from "the voice of authority: he spoke from firsthand knowledge of the law's failure to fulfill its promised protections for so many Americans."

Marshall especially hated the death penalty, which he felt was used disproportionately against non-white criminals. His Supreme Court clerks had strict orders to call him at any hour so he could support last-minute appeals from death row. When Chief Justice William Rehnquist once remarked that an inmate's appeals cost the system too much money, Marshall snapped: "It would have been cheaper to shoot him right after he was arrested, wouldn't it?"

Marshall was a passionate defender of free speech. In *Stanley v. Georgia* (1969), he ruled against censorship, even of pornography: "If the First Amendment means anything, it means that a state has no business telling a man, sitting alone in his own house, what books he may read or what films he may watch." He upheld the view that flag-burning is protected under the First Amendment, in a case argued by William Kunstler and described in this book. He was among the majority of justices to support the legalization of abortion in *Roe v. Wade* (1973).

However, Marshall was sometimes in the minority on key decisions. In those cases he wrote long, critical dissents. *San Antonio School District v. Rodriguez* (1973) was one of these cases. By a 5-4 vote, the Court upheld Texas's use of property taxes to fund public schools. Schools in richer areas would thus continue to have more resources. In effect, said Marshall, the decision barred blacks from an equal education—not by laws but by lack of money. There are still legal challenges on this issue.

As new and more conservative justices were appointed by Presidents Richard Nixon, Ronald Reagan, and George Bush, Marshall often found himself outnumbered.

> ❦ "I know my phone's been tapped regularly. And I don't care. Because all they're going to hear is my wife's gossiping and me cursing."

He suspected he was put under government surveillance in those years. Once a negotiator who could bring about unanimous decisions that carried maximum weight, he gradually became "The Great Dissenter." In particular, he grew furious whenever the Court overturned affirmative action programs.

One of his most passionate dissents came against *University of California Regents v. Bakke* (1978), which found it unconstitutional for a state-run medical school to set aside 16 percent of its first-year places for blacks and other minorities. "Bringing the Negro into the mainstream of American life should be a state interest of the highest order," Marshall declared. "To fail to do so is to insure that America will forever remain a divided society." In *Richmond v. Croson* (1989), which allowed Richmond, Virginia, to halt affirmative action for minority contractors, he accused his colleagues on the Court of "constitutionalizing [their] wishful thinking" that racial discrimination had ended.

For years Marshall refused interviews, saying his work spoke for him, but in 1987 he broke his silence. His long interview with Carl Rowan on public television was the first of many frank sessions with the press—highly unusual for sitting Supreme Court justices.

Marshall told Rowan that he ranked Ronald Reagan at "the bottom" as a president. He also said: "At this late date, I have come to the definite conclusion that if the U.S. is indeed the great melting pot, the Negro either didn't get in the pot or didn't get melted down." (Marshall used the terms "colored" and "Negro" all his life, only occasionally using "Afro-American" in his later years.) He assured Rowan that he still enjoyed "the fight" and would serve until "the end of my term—life."

In June 1991 heart disease, bronchitis, and glaucoma forced Marshall to retire. Warm tributes from the American Bar Association, *Ebony* magazine, and other sources soon followed. When asked how he would like to be remembered, Marshall said simply: "He did the best he could with what he had."

Reliably plain-spoken and down to earth, Thurgood Marshall was always popular with reporters. He stopped granting interviews, however, during his first 20 years on the Supreme Court.
(308-PSD671-981, National Archives)

Marshall died on January 24, 1993, at age 84. Tens of thousands of mourners came to pay their respects in the Great Hall of the Supreme Court, where he lay in state on the bier that had held Abraham Lincoln. Marshall was an active Episcopalian and was buried in a religious service.

Marshall was a giant in the field of civil rights and a courtroom pioneer long before his historic appointment to the Supreme Court. His friend and protégé, former U.S. Court of Appeals judge A. Leon Higginbotham, Jr., assessed his legacy this way: "But for Thurgood Marshall, this country would be torn asunder in ways you cannot imagine. He not only helped black people, he helped America become the nation it must someday become." Even Marshall's critics have agreed, in the words of the *Encyclopedia of American Biography*, "that his record as America's leading civil rights lawyer will not soon be surpassed."

Chronology

July 2, 1908	Thoroughgood Marshall born in Baltimore, Maryland; changes spelling of name to "Thurgood" as a boy
1929	marries Vivian (Buster) Burey
1930	graduates with honors from Lincoln University
1933	earns law degree from Howard University; starts private law practice in Baltimore
1935	joins the legal staff of the National Association for the Advancement of Colored People (NAACP)
1938–61	becomes lead lawyer for the NAACP's Legal Defense and Educational Fund
1944–50	successfully argues several racial discrimination cases before the Supreme Court
1951	investigates court-martials of black soldiers in Korea and Japan
1952–1954	leads defense team for *Brown v. Board of Education of Topeka,* the Supreme Court case that outlaws school desegregation
1955	Vivian Marshall dies; Thurgood Marshall marries Cecilia Suyat; they have two sons, Thurgood, Jr., and John William
1960	helps Kenya create its constitution
1961	appointed U.S. Circuit Court of Appeals judge
1965	appointed solicitor general

Thurgood Marshall

1967	appointed first black Supreme Court justice; serves until retiring in 1991
January 24, 1993	Thurgood Marshall dies

Further Reading

"'The Best I Could with What I Had:' The Legacy of Thurgood Marshall." *Ebony,* September 1991. Extensive photographic tribute with detailed captions, and a short biography.

Goldman, Roger, with David Gallen. *Thurgood Marshall: Justice for All.* New York: Carroll & Graf, 1992. Nontraditional three-part biography contains colleagues' views of Marshall, a law professor's view of his work, and excerpts from key Supreme Court opinions that Marshall wrote.

Hengstler, Gary A. "Looking Back: Reflections on a Life Well-Spent." *ABA Journal,* June 1992. Marshall talks frankly about American history, racism, and the milestones in his career. Full of interesting quotes.

"Thurgood Marshall." *Current Biography Yearbook,* 1989. Sketch of Marshall's life and career.

Haskins, James. *Thurgood Marshall: A Life for Justice.* New York: Henry Holt & Co., 1992. One of several good Marshall biographies for young readers.

Rowan, Carl T. *Dream Makers, Dream Breakers: The World of Justice Thurgood Marshall.* Boston: Little, Brown & Co., 1993. Rowan, a black journalist, wrote this full-length biography after interviewing Marshall in 1988 for a Public Broadcasting System documentary.

Wolters, Raymond. *The Burden of Brown: 30 Years of School Desegregation.* Knoxville: University of Tennessee Press, 1984. Case studies.

William Kunstler
(1919–1995)

*William Kunstler was proud to be a lawyer for civil rights
activists, vicious criminals, and social outcasts.*
(Law Offices of Kunstler & Kuby)

*W*as it a courtroom or a Marx Brothers movie set? A trial or
a farce? The defendants—a group of hippies, Yippies, and
pacifists dubbed the Chicago Seven—talked back to the
scolding old judge, blew kisses to the jury, and had a birthday
cake delivered to the bench. The Seven were accused of con-
spiring to riot at the 1968 Democratic National Convention.
To many Americans it seemed that the Woodstock-era youth
culture and anti-Vietnam war movement were on trial.

William Kunstler was a lawyer for the Chicago Seven. He
had been a civil rights activist; the trial of the Seven turned
him into a radical. "I threw down my polite lawyerly behavior

and took up the fighter's stance," he said. "I learned to fight fire with fire."

Once a liberal suburbanite who felt awkward raising his fist in a Black Power salute, "Wild Bill" Kunstler would transform himself into an outlaw who gleefully represented outlaws. Unlike many of the Chicago Seven, he would never stray from his devotion to radical causes. Even Kunstler's enemies—and he had many—could not deny his persistence.

William Moses Kunstler was born on July 7, 1919, in New York City, the adored first son of Frances and Monroe Kunstler. His father was a well–respected doctor whose income ensured a good living even during the Great Depression of the 1930s. His mother's father was also a doctor, physician to several New York sports teams and its mayors. Kunstler and his younger brother and sister grew up with a sense of their family's importance, living in a nine-room Upper West Side apartment and spending summers on Long Island or in rural Connecticut.

Although his parents were not political, Kunstler traced his passion for justice to those early years. "Coming from a family that had provided me with a childhood of comfort and security, I felt that in order to validate my life, my time on earth had to count for something," he explained.

Like other lawyers, including Clarence Darrow and Thurgood Marshall, as a boy Kunstler could neither sit still nor keep quiet in school. At 13 he joined a small-time street gang; he always recalled his joy at being "the only white kid among blacks and Hispanics," rebelling against his middle-class upbringing by smashing windows and taunting cops. Kunstler's love for books and poetry, and his underlying desire for his parents' approval, won out. He entered Yale University, majored in French, and planned a writing career.

The Kunstlers, however, saw their son as a future doctor. But while Kunstler was always highly physical—he was a tall, loping man who loved to touch and hug—he was not doctor material. "I dragged myself to operations by the score, including my brother's appendectomy, but finally I couldn't take it," Kunstler said. "The only way to get them off my back was to say 'I'll be a lawyer instead.'"

World War II intervened. After graduating from Yale, Kunstler joined the army and served in the Pacific under General Douglas MacArthur. He became a cryptologist, or code breaker, earning a Bronze Star for merit, and achieving the rank of major in only five years. Surprisingly, given his general contempt for authority, Kunstler loved the army—or at least the "adrenaline-surging, heart-pounding" aspects of his time in it. He also enjoyed giving orders, a trait that stayed with him throughout his life.

> ❦ "Initially I went to law school because it offered status, prestige, and the promise of a reasonably high income—all the wrong reasons."

The war years were eventful for Kunstler in other ways. While on leave in 1943, he married Lotte Rosenberger, a 17-year-old German refugee whom he knew from family get-togethers; they were distant cousins. Nine months and one day after their wedding, Karin Fernanda Kunstler was born.

After leaving the army in 1946, Kunstler put aside dreams of journalism and joined his brother, Michael, at Columbia Law School. The government paid his tuition—a fact he always chortled over—under the veteran's program known as the G.I. Bill of Rights. Kunstler supported his wife and daughter by writing hundreds of freelance book reviews for magazines, and selling law-course summaries to students one semester behind him. He also wrote the libretto, or script, for an opera based on Shirley Jackson's short story "The Lottery."

Admitted to the New York Bar in December 1948, Kunstler followed a path common to hundreds of thousands of young veterans. He took advantage of a no-money-down

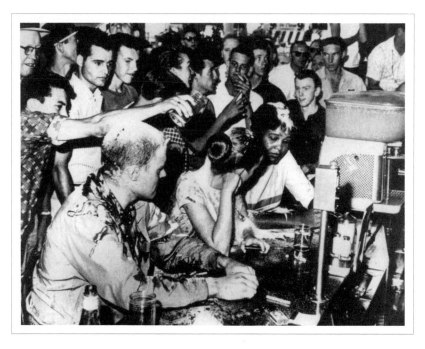

Lunch counter sit-in, Jackson, Mississippi, May 1963. Scenes like this, in which Freedom Riders were tormented by southerners who opposed racial integration, steered William Kunstler toward civil rights law.
(WHi-X3-36638, John Salter Collection, State Historical Society of Wisconsin)

G.I. mortgage to buy a home in the suburbs, enlarged his family—a second daughter, Jane, was born in 1949—and launched his career.

Kunstler's early legal work was routine. He and his brother set up a small practice in Manhattan, with Michael handling property matters, while Bill tended to divorces and occasional lawsuits. As an artistic outlet, Kunstler hosted radio shows in which he dramatized historic trials and commented on legal matters of the day—not unlike Court TV's current commentators.

The story of William Kunstler might have ended there, uneventful and American as an unburnt flag, had the civil rights movement not erupted in the 1960s. Previously, Kunstler had been what he called a "parlor liberal," somewhat active in the American Civil Liberties Union (ACLU) but hardly a crusader. Then, one incident transformed his life.

In May 1961, the Congress of Racial Equality (CORE) launched "freedom rides," in which blacks and whites rode together on buses and trains to challenge segregation laws that still applied to interstate travel in the South. With waves of freedom riders being arrested and jailed, the ACLU asked Kunstler to meet with CORE's overworked lawyers. Kunstler reluctantly agreed; he sympathized with the cause but did not care to spend a hot summer in the Deep South.

Arriving in Jackson, Mississippi, Kunstler almost immediately witnessed the violent arrest of five young Freedom Riders as they sat down at a bus terminal lunch counter. The scene imprinted itself like a religious vision. Awed by the "total human commitment" of the protesters, he felt his own comfortable life to be a sham.

A few weeks before his 42nd birthday, William Kunstler was reborn as a civil rights activist. Working with CORE, he dusted off an 1866 law called the removal statute, and put it to bold use. Originally created to protect newly freed slaves from courts controlled by their former masters, this statute forced federal courts to remove certain cases from state courts, and required them to set reasonable bail. Kunstler would invoke the statute in the state courts whenever freedom riders were arrested, immediately winning their release. It became a legal lever that helped ensure survival for the civil rights movement.

In a sense, Kunstler never looked back. After Mississippi he plunged nonstop into civil rights, representing and befriending Martin Luther King, Jr., Harlem politician Adam Clayton Powell, black militants Stokely Carmichael and H. Rap Brown, and numerous lesser-known activists.

Chicago, August 1968. Armed soldiers formed a barricade against hippies who had come to protest the Vietnam War during the Democratic presidential convention. The Chicago Seven were accused of inciting the protesters to riot.
(LCU9-19773-24, U.S. News and World Report Collection, Library of Congress)

One of his favorite cases was a little-publicized coup worthy of Thurgood Marshall. In *Hobson v. Hansen,* Kunstler won a federal court ruling against a "track system" that had relegated black children in the desegregated schools of Washington, D.C., to an inferior education.

"For a while I had the idea that this was kind of the white man's burden, coming down to help the struggling blacks in the South, which I realize now was a horrible, condescending attitude to have," Kunstler later said. His work in what he called "people's law" was not confined to black causes. He defended white Roman Catholic peace militants Daniel and Philip Berrigan, who registered moral opposition to the Vietnam War by destroying Selective Service military draft records. As the war escalated, Kunstler plunged into what is perhaps his most famous case—defending the Chicago Seven.

A decade's worth of heated politics and emotions boiled over in Chicago in August 1968. About 10,000 young people had descended on the city for a week to demonstrate at the Democratic National Convention, where the presidential nomination and seemingly the course of the Vietnam War was up for grabs. Leading candidate Robert F. Kennedy had been assassinated two months earlier, and President Lyndon B. Johnson withdrew from the race.

The week had its lighter moments. For example, when members of the Youth International Party—better known as Yippies—introduced a piglet named Pigasus as their presidential choice. Unlike Woodstock, the legendary gathering of the previous summer, Chicago turned violent. "The whole world is watching!" demonstrators chanted as television cameras recorded their bloody clashes with law enforcement officers.

A federal commission later judged the confrontations a "police riot," but those arrested as the perpetrators were eight radicals. They were accused of crossing state lines to incite riots. The law under which they were charged was written a year earlier, during a summer of race riots in many U.S. cities. They were also charged with criminal conspiracy, despite the fact that some had never met each other before their arrest.

At first they were the Chicago Eight: Abbie Hoffman and Jerry Rubin, Yippie leaders; David Dellinger, pacifist head of the National Mobilization Against the War; Tom Hayden and Rennie Davis, leaders of the left-wing Students for a Democratic Society; Lee Weiner and John Froines, teachers and activists; and Bobby Seale, cofounder of the Black Panther Party. According to legal historian Colin Evans, their five-month trial would become "possibly the most divisive—certainly the most

"Don't give into oppression; make fun of it."

chaotic—political trial in American history." Hoffman's opening statement set the stage: "My name is Abbie," he intoned, hand on Bible. "I am an orphan of America . . . I live in Woodstock Nation."

The case was a natural for Kunstler and co-counsel Leonard Weinglass. Nonetheless, Bobby Seale disavowed them and tried to lead his own defense. Presiding over this show within a show was 73-year-old Judge Julius J. Hoffman (no relation to Abbie Hoffman), who was openly hostile to the defendants. When Judge Hoffman ordered the disruptive Seale to be bound and gagged, Kunstler leapt up protesting "medieval torture." Seale was tied to his chair for three days, until the judge declared Seale's case a mistrial, leaving seven defendants—the Chicago Seven.

The war between the Chicago Seven and Judge Hoffman was a running theme of the trial. They made trouble; he issued warnings and contempt citations fast and furiously; that encouraged them. The defendants' attitude emboldened Kunstler. When prosecutors brought in police officers to bolster their case, Kunstler invited performers and writers as expert witnesses on youth culture and the antiwar movement. Phil Ochs, Judy Collins, and Arlo Guthrie sang until courtroom marshals stopped them; poet Allen Ginsberg chanted *Ommmmmmm* on the stand. There were many theatrical exchanges, like this one, between bench and bar:

Judge Hoffman: *This is not a political case.*

Kunstler: *It is quite a political case.*

Judge Hoffman: *It is a criminal case.*

Kunstler: *Your Honor, Jesus was accused criminally, too, and we understand really that was not truly a criminal case in the sense that it is just an ordinary...*

Judge Hoffman [interrupting]: *I didn't live at that time.*

Kunstler: *Well, I was assuming Your Honor had read of the incident.*

On February 20, 1970, all the defendants except Froines and Weiner were found guilty. They were freed on appeal in 1972, with the appellate court basing its reversal on Judge Hoffman's procedural errors and "antagonistic attitude." In addition, the Chicago Seven, along with Kunstler and Weinglass, had been sentenced to prison on contempt charges. These citations were also overturned, but not easily.

According to historian Terry H. Anderson, writing 25 years after the trial in his book *The Movement and the Sixties*:

> *Justice was not the point of the [Chicago Seven] trial; it was detention, an attempt to curtail the activists by legal wrangling that eventually cost them and their supporters half a million dollars during the next five years before the case was thrown out of court. During that time the government kept them under surveillance and harassed them. . . . In one five-week period [Abbie] Hoffman was questioned once by the Internal Revenue Service, twice by the Justice Department, and five times by the FBI. While he sat in jail, the sheriff ordered his head shaved and displayed the long mane as a trophy.*

Many critics would have loved to lock up and scalp "Wild Bill" Kunstler as well. The American Bar Association did not comment directly on the Chicago Seven case, but a June 1970 editorial in the *ABA Journal* took Kunstler to task for declaring that he would accept as clients "only those whose goals I share." Conservative publisher William F. Buckley was more forthright. In his magazine, *National Review*, he wrote: "Kunstler should be disbarred." Buckley's brother James, then a U.S. senator from New York, was so enraged by his state's refusal to disbar Kunstler that he drafted a law that would have empowered the U.S. Justice Department to discipline lawyers. The attempt failed.

Contempt citations flew thick and fast over the years, but while Kunstler was publicly censured (reprimanded) for his courtroom conduct, he was never convicted of contempt. To him, each rebuke was a badge of honor.

Mississippi changed Kunstler, but Chicago revolutionized him. Chicago was where Clarence Darrow taught himself to put society, not the criminal, on trial; it was where Kunstler learned to put America's judicial system, not the criminal, on trial. The case and its aftermath stripped Kunstler's last vestiges of what he called "middle-class faith" in that system.

"In Chicago, in the same type of federal court I had relied on for years, I was suddenly confronted by a tyrannical judge, malicious prosecutors, and lying witnesses. . . . To this day, I have not gotten over it," Kunstler wrote at age 75 in *My Life as a Radical Lawyer.* "It taught me the hardest lesson of my life: The judicial system in this country is often unjust and will punish those whom it hates or fears." He held a special hatred for the Federal Bureau of Investigation for its "routine destruction of dissident organizations and individuals."

The Chicago Seven case made Kunstler a national celebrity, a role he adored. He used his fame to change his practice. By charging high fees for lectures, and drawing a small but steady salary from the Center for Constitutional Rights, a legal organization he co-founded, Kunstler was able to accept more radical cases *pro bono,* at no cost to the client.

In the 1970s, Kunstler championed several high-profile causes. He rushed to Attica Correctional Facility in upstate New York when its inmates staged a riot and held guards hostage. The insurrection lasted four days and left thirty-nine people dead; most of that time, Kunstler was inside the prison yard, acting as the inmates' negotiator.

Kunstler was afraid at first to enter Attica. His response shows how he felt about physical fear: "In my mind, I prepared to have my throat cut. I intellectualized that it shouldn't hurt much; it would be over quickly. But if I ran, I would always be remembered as a coward." He told himself much the same thing whenever he received death threats, which was fairly often.

The Attica inmates welcomed Kunstler, as did another disenfranchised group he represented in the 1970s, the

American Indian Movement (AIM). To protest the plight of Indian life on government reservations, AIM and other Native American groups staged a siege in 1973 at Wounded Knee, South Dakota, where U.S. Cavalry troops had brutally massacred Sioux Indians in 1890. Just as he had immersed himself in the world of civil rights workers,

> ❦ "Every time I have a different case, I want to be the color or race. I want to be Indians. Sikhs I want to be. Blacks I want to be."

Yippies, and prisoners, Kunstler plunged enthusiastically into the Native American activist culture.

In several different cases stemming from the siege at Wounded Knee, Kunstler tried to do for the Sioux what Belva Lockwood had done for the Cherokees decades before: force the U.S. government to make reparations for lands seized from the Indians long ago, often under false treaties. He successfully defended several Sioux leaders who were accused, like the Chicago Seven, of criminal conspiracy against the government, winning freedom for three out of four Sioux who were charged with murdering a pair of FBI agents. In 17 years of appeals, however, Kunstler never managed to reverse the life sentence of the fourth alleged murderer in that case, Leonard Peltier.

During the early 1970s, Kunstler's first marriage ended. For years he and his wife, Lotte, had shared the same politics and devotion to their children, but little else. In 1975 Kunstler wed Margaret Ratner, a progressive lawyer he had met on a case, and in his late 50s became a father again. His deep affection for both sets of daughters—Karin, a lawyer; Jane, a physician; and college students Sarah and Emily— was unmistakable. All four have been active in left-wing causes and protests. Kunstler often recounted their first arrests as proudly as other fathers might have recalled a child's first step.

In 1982, Kunstler began working closely with Ronald Kuby, whom he called "my partner and my alter ego." Some observers said that Kuby was the son Kunstler never had. Kuby says he's quite happy with his real father, but his affection for his employer was clear. He is dedicated to carrying on Kunstler's mission of representing society's outcasts.

Lawyers at the Center for Constitutional Rights were also an extended family for Kunstler. His longtime affiliation with the Center led to his involvement in *Texas v. Johnson,* the major flag-burning case of the 1980s. This case was tailor-made for Kunstler, given his equal passions for the Constitution and the grand gesture.

The *cause célèbre* began in 1984, when Gregory Lee "Joey" Johnson protested the policies of President Ronald Reagan by setting a flag on fire outside the Republican National Convention in Dallas. Johnson was promptly arrested. The appeals court in Dallas County upheld his conviction, but a state appeals court overturned it. The state of Texas appealed the case to the Supreme Court, where Kunstler argued it on March 21, 1989.

Even Bill Kunstler toned down his delivery and slicked back his long, steel-woolish gray hair for his appearances before the high court. His goal, of course, was to win, and so he played by the rules—using strategies not unlike those used by conservative lawyer John W. Davis in his many Supreme Court arguments.

"My method was to use precedents, many of which had been written by the justices themselves," Kunstler said. "I made my point that the person who burned the flag did not intend to do anything other than exercise his right to free speech." He told the Court:

> To hear things or to see things that we hate tests the First Amendment more than seeing or hearing things that we like. It wasn't designed for things we like. They never needed a First Amendment for that.

The Supreme Court agreed, voting 6-3 in Johnson's favor. "We can imagine no more appropriate response to burning a flag than waving one's own," said Justice William J. Brennan in the majority decision. "We do not consecrate the flag by punishing its desecration, for in doing so we dilute the freedom that this cherished emblem represents."

Many flag-loving Americans loudly disagreed. Under angry public pressure, Congress quickly passed the Flag Protection Act of 1989. Just as quickly—indeed, on the day that act became law—Joey Johnson and others took out their matches to test it. Two new flag-burning cases arose and the issue returned to the Supreme Court in 1990, where Kunstler again argued and won for Johnson.

> ❦ "While I have not found a better system, I cannot approve of ours and do not take part in many of its rituals. For example, I never stand for the Pledge of Allegiance, because . . . the United States does not provide 'justice for all.'"

Yet this deeply symbolic issue will not rest. Periodically, lawmakers introduce a constitutional amendment that would decide the legality of flag burning once and for all. As of early 1996, no such amendment had passed.

In his later years Kunstler gravitated toward clients whom, he admitted, "do not have the same moral stature in the eyes of the community" as the civil rights leaders and antiwar activists he once championed; many were charged with extremely violent felonies. Among them were the Islamic terrorists found guilty of bombing New York City's World Trade Center; Larry Davis, acquitted on charges of murdering nine New York City policemen; and Yusef Salaam, one of the young men accused of rape and attempted murder in the Central Park jogger case—for which Linda Fairstein handled the prosecution's trial strategy. In a brief connection he called "the odd couple," Kunstler represented organized crime kingpin John Gotti.

Kunstler lost no sleep over the guilt or innocence of these or other clients. "I think it's ethically correct to defend someone whom I believe is guilty," he said. "Otherwise only the innocent would have lawyers." What mattered to him was to be allied with his client's cause. That is why Kunstler and Kuby did not, for example, consider defending Timothy McVeigh, the chief suspect in the Oklahoma City bombing episode in early 1995.

Kunstler's principles also lost him the support of likely friends. The Jewish Defense League picketed Kunstler's New York City home and office when he represented El Sayyid Nasair, the accused killer of Rabbi Meir Kahane. A rape survivor who once respected Kunstler says that his "groveling defense" of Yusef Salaam "convinced me that he is a sickening old man who loves publicity and scum, in that order." Helen Engelhardt, whose husband Tony Hawkins was one of 259 passengers killed by a terrorist-planted bomb on Pan Am Flight 103 in 1988, said:

> It wasn't Kunstler's alacrity in defending Arab terrorists, but his 'black rage' defense of Long Island railway killer Colin Ferguson that pushed him off the map for me. Kunstler no longer seemed able to distinguish between people who were genuine victims of prejudice and fear because of their unpopular ideas, and people who were murderers. Unlike Darrow, who did not rationalize Leopold and Loeb's behavior, but questioned the wisdom of the death penalty, Kunstler actually tried to justify why Ferguson felt compelled to kill six innocent people and injure 19 others. Based on the entire arc of his career, however, I think Kunstler was an admirable and even precious resource.

Public opinion, good or bad, meant little to Kunstler. In a 1994 public forum with two other high-profile defense lawyers, Alan M. Dershowitz and Barry I. Slotnick, he managed to provoke even a sophisticated audience at the 92nd Street YMCA in New York City with this interchange:

Kunstler: *I wouldn't have taken O. J. Simpson as a client because I don't take spousal murder cases.*

Slotnick: Difficult for me to believe, because O. J. Simpson as a black man fits into a bit of a pattern for Bill Kunstler.

Kunstler: I didn't think O. J. was black. [Here the audience gasped.] From his life style? No, he is not a black man in the tradition of black people I have taken.

Moderator: That's a broad stereotype.

Kunstler: I know it is, but his life style was a white life style.

At that the crowd hissed, but Kunstler remained unruffled.

Kunstler died of cardiac arrest at age 76 after a short illness. Barely a month before he died, he fulfilled a dream—he performed as a stand-up comic at a popular Manhattan comedy club.

Will William Kunstler go down in legal history as a key advocate for civil and constitutional rights, or as the eternal bad boy of American law? Perhaps the most perceptive view came from Jeffrey Rosen, legal affairs editor of *The New Republic,* in his review of Kunstler's autobiography, *My Life as a Radical Lawyer:*

> *Compared to the current generation of self-promoting celebrity advocates, at least [Kunstler] has never been mercenary. He has devoted dark and lonely hours, many of them without pay, to the most difficult and unpopular cases. But there is something sad and emblematic about his evolution from the charismatic civil libertarian of the Lyndon Johnson era to the racial provocateur of today. His career is a metaphor for the polarization of racial politics in the U.S. over the last 30 years.*

Writing his own epitaph, Kunstler expressed no regrets about anything. "In whatever future I have," he said not long before dying, "I will continue to do exactly what I have done since I first entered that bus terminal in Jackson, Mississippi in 1961. . . . I would like to be remembered as someone who did what I wanted to do with my life. And who contributed, in some way or another, to the holding on to whatever rights and liberties are still available to Americans."

Chronology

▬▬▬▬▬▬▬

July 7, 1919	William Moses Kunstler born in New York, New York
1941	receives B.A. from Yale University
1941–46	serves in U.S. Army in World War II; marries Lotte Rosenberger (1943) and begins raising a family
1948	earns law degree from Columbia University Law School; is admitted to the New York Bar
1948–74	with his brother, is a partner in the New York City law firm of Kunstler & Kunstler
1961–69	devotes himself to civil rights causes; co-founds the Center for Constitutional Rights (1969)
1969–70	is co-counsel for the Chicago Seven
1971–95	continues to defend numerous controversial clients; divorces Lotte Kunstler; marries Margaret Ratner (1975) and has a second family
1989–90	argues flag-burning case twice before the Supreme Court
September 4, 1995	William Kunstler dies

Further Reading

Anderson, Terry H. *The Movement and the Sixties: Protest in America from Greensboro to Wounded Knee.* New York: Oxford University Press, 1995. This impressively detailed history of the protest movement puts Kunstler's career into full context.

Evory, Ann, editor. "William M(oses) Kunstler." In *Contemporary Authors: New Revision Series, Volume 5.* Detroit: Gale Research, 1982. A short, insightful biography and interview.

Goldberg, Stephanie B. "Lessons of the 60's." *American Bar Association Journal,* May 15, 1987. Discusses legal consequences of the Chicago Seven trial and others of the 1960s.

Jacoby, Tamar. "A Fight for Old Glory." *Newsweek,* July 3, 1989. Summarizes the Supreme Court's first decision on flag burning.

Kunstler, William with Sheila Isenberg. *My Life as a Radical Lawyer.* New York: Carol Publishing Group/Birch Lane Press, 1994. Kunstler reviews his life and career in short episodes that reflect his humor, outrage, and thirst for controversy.

Leinwand, Gerald, Ph.D. *Freedom of Speech.* New York: Facts On File, 1991. Part of the "American Issues" series for young adults. Reviews the history and issues surrounding this basic right.

F. Lee Bailey
(1933–)

F. Lee Bailey was selected for O. J. Simpson's defense team because he built his career by defending men accused of killing their wives.
(Law Offices of F. Lee Bailey)

Do you remember where you were on the night on June 17, 1994?

O. J. Simpson remembers, although he was never called to testify about it at his criminal trial. That was the night he learned he was under suspicion for the death of his ex-wife, Nicole Brown Simpson, and her friend, Ronald L. Goldman.

That was the night of the infamous "white Bronco," when Simpson resisted arrest by taking to the freeways in a Ford truck while an amazed country watched the chase on television.

F. Lee Bailey remembers, too. He was at home in West Palm Beach, Florida, and his lawyer's intuition told him that the unfolding Simpson drama would explode into the one of most notorious cases of the century. He had already been involved in more than a few such cases, and he couldn't wait to get his hands on this one.

Francis Lee Bailey was born in Waltham, Massachusetts, on June 10, 1933. He dislikes his first name, and has always been called Lee.

The boy who would become one of America's toughest criminal defense lawyers grew up on the well-manicured grounds of a nursery school. His mother, Grace, founded the school and ran it until her retirement. Bailey has always been close to his hardworking mother; at age 15, he walked her down the aisle at her second wedding and "gave her away," at her request. He has never had much to say about his father, an advertising salesman who left his wife and three children when Lee was ten.

Like some other teachers' children, including Thurgood Marshall, Bailey was not a model student. As a teenager he was sent to boarding school in New Hampshire, where he channeled his energies into writing. He did well enough to get into Harvard, but the Ivy League bored him. Bailey left Harvard after two years to join the navy; he liked boating, and he was itching to learn to fly.

> ❦ "I'll never forget the eighth grade shop teacher who told my mother that he'd keep me sanding a block of wood until I learned to do it his way, if it took all year. It took all year, but I still did it my way."

The rigors of military life and the thrill of flight training suited Bailey just fine—so well, in fact, that he transferred to the Marines to get more flying time. Bailey was then thinking about a legal career, and volunteered for the unpopular post of second assistant legal officer. (All branches of the U.S. Armed Forces have their own courts and rules of law.) Soon he was promoted to chief legal officer at his base in North Carolina.

During 18 months in the military courts, Bailey was involved in some 200 cases, ranging from theft to wife-beating. Off-duty, he moonlighted as a private detective for a local civilian lawyer, which taught him the value of pre-trial legwork. These apprenticeships turned Bailey into a critic of standard legal education; he still rails at law schools for their lack of real-world training.

Though Bailey may have left the Marines feeling like a real lawyer, he couldn't practice law back home in Massachusetts without a degree. Boston University Law School accepted him on the basis of his military work and two years at Harvard. On the same day Bailey entered Boston University, he opened a private detective agency that did investigations for lawyers. One motive was his need for money; by now Bailey was a married man with two sons. He also loved detective work, and it helped him make connections among working lawyers that gave him a jump on his fellow graduates.

One connection in particular paid off quickly. Less than a month after being admitted to the Massachusetts Bar in 1960, a lawyer Bailey knew called him about a lurid, headline-grabbing murder case. It was called the "Torso Murder" because the search for the victim—a woman allegedly killed by her husband—turned up a headless body.

Bailey was summoned because, at the time, he was one of the few polygraph specialists in Massachusetts. Polygraph machines are lie detectors—or truth verifiers, as Bailey prefers to call them. They chart a person's "involuntary" reactions to crucial questions by measuring changes in blood pressure, pulse, breathing, and skin response. A few decades ago these tests were as common as DNA tests are today. Their scientific accuracy was always disputed, however, and polygraphic evidence is no longer admissible in court.

Bailey used polygraph reports to bolster the case of the Torso Murderer. He also took over the trial and won an acquittal when the leading lawyer fell ill. Thus, F. Lee Bailey's first civilian trials splashed him onto the front pages—and launched his reputation as *the* lawyer to call if accused of killing your wife.

The following year, 1961, Bailey was called again to work his magic on behalf of Sam Sheppard, an Ohio doctor seven years into a life sentence for killing his wife. Sheppard's 1954 trial was as publicized and sensational as the O. J. Simpson trial in the 1990s. *The New York Times* called it "a Roman circus." In Sheppard's case, however, the media hype was stirred up mainly by the judge, who shamelessly sought publicity because he was running for reelection.

In his badger-like way, Bailey burrowed into the case. After poring over 9,808 pages of case history, and filing two years' worth of retrial requests, he got Sheppard freed on bail. The appellate judge said that the doctor's original trial had been so circus-like that it "fell far below the minimum requirements for due process."

Bailey pressed Sheppard's case upward to the Supreme Court, where it made legal history in 1966. The justices agreed that, in 1954, Sheppard had been tried and found guilty in the press, rather than the courtroom. Specifically, they claimed that the original judge "did not fulfill his duty to protect Sheppard from inherently prejudicial publicity which saturated the country." Judges, they charged, have a responsibility to do whatever is necessary—to sequester jurors, curtail grandstanding by lawyers, postpone or move a trial—in order to ensure the constitutional right to a fair trial. This ruling still weighs heavily on judges. Clearly it was behind criticism of Simpson trial Judge Lance A. Ito as,

> ❦ "Even in casual conversation, criminal [defense] lawyers do not like to lose."

according to *New York Times* reporter David Margolick, "a too tolerant judge too reluctant to assert control, then too arbitrary when he finally does."

Thanks to Bailey, Sam Sheppard won the right to be retried, and was found innocent. Although Sheppard soon died, he lived on as the inspiration for the television show "The Fugitive." His case lives on, having raised issues and set precedents that have new meaning in the era of television trial coverage.

The irony is that Bailey was a creature of publicity. He emerged as *the* celebrity lawyer of the 1960s and 1970s, and he lived like one, in a 16-room mansion on a Massachusetts estate with an indoor pool, a landing pad for the helicopters he loved to pilot, and a succession of younger wives. Reporters were routinely invited to profile his lavish lifestyle. Bailey even equipped his office with television lights to be ready for cameras at a moment's notice.

Bailey often juggled cases in a dozen different states. He flew from trial to trial, piloting his own jet. One of Bailey's most notorious clients in the 1960s was Carl Coppolino, an anesthesiologist accused of murdering his ex-lover's husband and his own wife.

In a strategy worthy of Clarence Darrow, Bailey shifted attention away from his client and onto a scapegoat— namely Marjorie Farber, Coppolino's ex-lover, whom he had since dropped for a new paramour. Farber said Coppolino had hypnotized her into attempting to kill her husband; the prosecution said that Coppolino had injected the man with a deadly poison. Bailey managed to convince the jury that Marjorie Farber was lying and that her husband died naturally from a heart attack.

Some male lawyers of the 1960s continued to behave in a gentlemanly manner toward female witnesses. Not Bailey. From his opening statement onward, he tore into Farber:

This woman drips with venom on the inside, and I hope before we are through you will see it drip on the outside. She [still] wants [Carl Coppolino] so badly that she would sit on his lap in the electric chair. . . . This is not a murder case at all. This is monumental and shameful proof that hell hath no fury like a woman scorned.

The jury agreed. However, in a separate trial a few months later for the murder of his wife, Coppolino was convicted. In these back-to-back "love triangle" trials involving the same man, not even F. Lee Bailey could win two acquittals.

Soon Bailey was handling another case for the history books: the defense of Albert DeSalvo, the "Boston Strangler." Arrested for armed robbery and sexual assault, and suspected of perpetrating a grisly series of murders and rapes, DeSalvo was judged schizophrenic and held for two years in a state hospital. His mental status raised many legal complexities. Was DeSalvo insane? A cunning liar? Had he befriended the real "Boston Strangler" in the asylum, as some people believed, and wildly claimed another criminal's story as his own?

No one will ever know, but in 1967 the state decided DeSalvo *was* mentally competent and put him on trial. Bailey's task was not to prove his client innocent, for DeSalvo had never pretended to be, but "merely" insane, and in desperate need of treatment. However, the prosecution successfully convinced the jury that DeSalvo was a schemer and a "con," a vicious and guilty criminal.

After escaping from jail within a month—throwing Massachusetts into sheer terror for 24 hours until he was recaptured—DeSalvo was clapped into maximum security. A fellow inmate killed him in 1973. In Bailey's memoir *For the Defense,* published eight years after the trial, his bitterness about this case remained fresh:

DeSalvo should have been made the object of the most intensive medical and psychological testing known to modern science. Instead he was locked up and forgotten. Now we would never

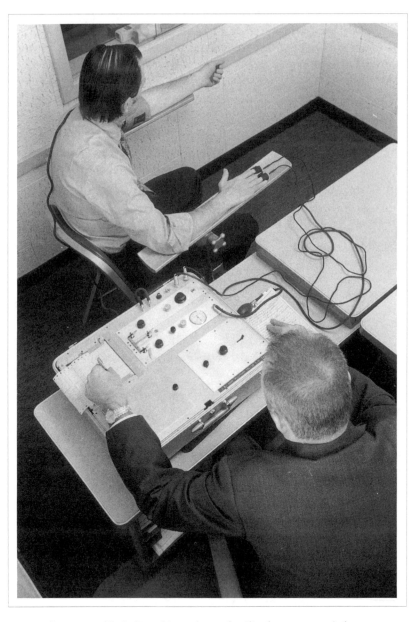

*Bailey staunchly believed in polygraphs (lie detector tests), but was
unable to use them effectively during the Medina trial.*
(LCU9-25517-15A, U.S. News and World Report Collection, Library of Congress)

*know just what combination of mistakes produced such a hor-
rendously warped mind—and so many terrible killings.*

From time to time people wondered how Bailey could
afford to represent clients like Albert DeSalvo, who are far
from rich. Like most lawyers, he budgets for some *pro bono*
work. However, Bailey has used another ploy. In most of his
high-profile cases, although not the O. J. Simpson case, he
controlled the sale of the book and/or movie rights until his
fees were fully paid.

The 1970s were a roller coaster for Bailey. His profession
punished him for being too much of a publicity hound by
censuring him publicly in Massachusetts, and suspending
him from practice for a year in New Jersey. Bailey's reply was
that talking to the press about cases was necessary "to balance
the record and at least keep the presumption of innocence
alive."

Soon, moreover, Bailey was the one on trial. In 1973 he
was indicted for mail fraud with a former client, Glenn W.
Turner, who he called "the hottest cosmetics salesman since
Eve talked Adam into a fig leaf." Although the case was eventually thrown out of court, it took a large toll on Bailey's time,
money, and status.

In the 1970s Bailey mounted a dedicated defense of U.S.
Army Captain Ernest L. Medina. On March 16, 1968,
Medina's troops killed more than 500 residents of the
Vietnamese village of My Lai. The dead included babies, children, and old people. No one slaughtered was either an
enemy soldier or armed. Photographs of the My Lai
Massacre were beamed around the world, and America hung
its head in shame. Opinion in the United States was already
heated and divisive about Vietnam, but few could condone
this carnage—not in the country that prided itself for vigor-
ously prosecuting similar war crimes at the Nürnberg Trials.

Medina was tried in army courts under the "Uniform Code
of Military Justice," which ex–Marine Bailey knew well.
Waiving his right to free army counsel, Medina had a military

stipend of $79 to hire an outsider. Bailey accepted it to repay a "debt of honor" to the military, where he felt he had been well trained in matters of law.

Army investigation into the incident pointed the chief blame at Lieutenant William L. Calley, a platoon leader under Captain Medina. Indeed, in 1970–71, Calley was tried and found guilty of 22 premeditated murders at My Lai. Calley unsuccessfully attempted the defense that Robert Jackson had forbidden to the Nazi defendants at Nürnberg. He claimed that he was just following orders—Medina's orders.

Bailey's defense strategy was simple. He said there was no evidence that Medina had ordered the wholesale killings or even been aware of them. Speaking for many observers, *Newsweek* magazine said that Bailey "turned his client into his own best witness." A quiet conservative of Mexican-American heritage, and a devoted army man, Medina came across as highly believable. He testified that Calley's platoon had made the first moves into My Lai. As Medina caught up, he said, he was so appalled by the number of dead bodies that he radioed ahead to cease fire.

Bailey called nine witnesses, all ex-members of Medina's unit. Not one placed him near the killings. One man testified that army investigators had tried to get him to incriminate Medina. Naturally, army prosecutors also called witnesses who were ex-soldiers. Some were also ex-drug users. With them, Bailey's cross-examinations took on an *Alice in Wonderland* quality:

> **Bailey:** *Have you been blowing any LSD lately?*
>
> **Former Army private Gerry Hemming:** *No, but I wish I could. Maybe it would make me forget this thing.*

William L. Calley was called as a defense witness. Although he had already been tried, he took the Fifth Amendment—refusing to testify because he might incriminate himself. That was a break for Medina, as was the appearance of an ex-soldier who said he had killed a boy that Medina was accused of killing. He was driven to come forward, he said, by a guilty conscience.

The Medina trial had some classic Bailey touches. At various times, Bailey petitioned the army to drop the trial on the basis of

> 🐦 "I believe cases are won by the lawyer who makes the fewest mistakes."

Medina's lie detector tests, which cleared him of the main charges. While military courts had a history of relying on polygraphy, this gambit failed. Following a television report that implied incompetence on the part of the judge, Bailey asked the judge to step down (motion denied) and then motioned for a mistrial (also denied). In the end, the so-called incompetent judge did Bailey and Medina a huge favor; he instructed the jury that in the killing of the civilians, Medina could be convicted only of involuntary manslaughter, a lesser charge than murder, because of insufficient evidence of intent to kill.

Years of agony for Captain Medina ended in a jury deliberation of just 57 minutes. The verdict was not guilty. Medina, nonetheless, resigned from his beloved army, feeling he would never again fit in. He began a new career with the Enstrom Helicopter Company at the invitation of its owner—F. Lee Bailey.

"I prefer cases that offer whopping fees and/or professional challenge," Bailey freely admitted in his book *The Defense Never Rests.* These preferences suggest why he agreed to defend Patricia Hearst, a media heiress and college student, in one of the most bizarre cases of the 1970s. It wasn't Bailey's typical kind of case, and it dealt quite a blow to his reputation.

Hearst was on trial for the armed robbery of a bank. Winning her case should have been easy. This young woman hardly fit the typical profile of a felon; she came from one of America's richest families. Her father was Randolph Hearst, owner of *The San Francisco Examiner.* Her grandfather was William Randolph Hearst, founder of the Hearst media empire, and the model for the larger-than-life newspaper mogul in the movie *Citizen Kane*. While Patty Hearst had taken part in bank robbery, it was not by choice.

The robbery occurred a few months after Hearst had been kidnapped at gunpoint by a politically radical, violent fringe group called the Symbionese Liberation Army (SLA). They targeted her because her father was "a corporate enemy of the people." SLA members hid Hearst, renamed her "Tania," and forced her under threat of death to do their criminal bidding. Despite constant efforts by the FBI to locate her, and by Randolph Hearst to ransom her, she ended up remaining in captivity for 20 months.

Bailey's strategy was to compare Patty Hearst to a prisoner of war. An army of psychiatric experts testified that Hearst had been brainwashed. Prosecutors countered with a slightly far-fetched theory. Patty was a sheltered rich girl who hadn't tried to escape the SLA because she loved her new role as a rebel.

It was widely expected that Hearst would go free, but the case seemed to self-destruct during closing arguments. The prosecutor was tightly focused, while Bailey rambled. "I could see that his hands were shaking," Hearst recalled in her book *Every Secret Thing*. Midway in the speech, Bailey gestured with his arm and spilled water down the front of his pants. He ignored it and went on speaking, Hearst said, "of people eating each other in the Andes, of G. Gordon Liddy, of the plot of a book called *A Covenant with Death*, and he talked at length about himself and the difficult tasks of lawyers." Bailey's most straightforward plea to the jury was: "Patricia Hearst was not a bad girl."

Prison was Hearst's next destination. Three years later, in 1979, President Jimmy Carter responded to public outcry and commuted (ended) her sentence. Although Bailey had carefully secured exclusive rights to write the first book about the Hearst case, he never wrote one, although he spent a good part of the 1980s coauthoring textbooks for lawyers and writing a courtroom novel.

F. Lee Bailey

O. J. Simpson hired a "dream team" of attorneys to defend him. Bailey's controversial cross-examination of former Los Angeles police detective Mark Fuhrman was a turning point in the case.
(Marian Calabro)

For several years, F. Lee Bailey faded from the public eye. The Hearst loss was only one reason. Many important cases were going to a new crop of celebrity lawyers like Alan Dershowitz, the Harvard law professor who assisted Bailey with strategy on the Hearst case. Bailey also experienced an arrest in 1982 for drunk driving. Robert Shapiro, a prominent California lawyer, successfully handled his defense, and the two men became close friends.

Shortly after O. J. Simpson was arrested as the prime suspect in the death of his former wife Nicole and her friend Ronald L. Goldman, he chose Robert Shapiro as his lead lawyer. Shapiro in turn chose Bailey to be part of Simpson's multi-lawyer "dream team."

Some saw it as Bailey's chance for a comeback, but he was rarely in the limelight. Still a staunch believer in detective work, he oversaw a team of private investigators who tracked down and computer-cataloged literally everything related to *California v. Orenthal James Simpson,* from the floor plans of Nicole Brown Simpson's home at 875 South Bundy Drive to every tabloid snippet about the case. Roger E. Sandler in *Life* magazine called Bailey the "organizer and supervisor of the kind of day-to-day scut work that can make the difference between winning and losing a murder trial."

From the opening arguments on January 24, 1995, the televised trial was sensationalized and as avidly viewed as any fictional drama or soap opera. Simpson's houseguest Brian "Kato" Kaelin, who testified to the suspect's whereabouts on the night of the crime, became an instant celebrity, as did Denise Brown, Nicole Brown Simpson's sister, who gave emotional testimony. The bloody glove found at O. J. Simpson's Brentwood estate a few hours after the murders, DNA testing, alleged racial strife among the sequestered jurors—these and many lesser elements permeated the nation's psyche. Americans became intensely familiar with prosecutors Marcia Clark and Christopher Darden, as well as Johnnie L. Cochran, Jr., Gerald Uelman, DNA specialist Barry Scheck, and others in Simpson's small army of lawyers.

F. Lee Bailey, however, was the lawyer who raised television ratings—and eyebrows—to new heights during his three-day cross-examination of Detective Mark Fuhrman. The defense hypothesis was that the former Los Angeles Police Department detective had framed Simpson by planting that infamous bloody glove at his home. Why would he do that? Because, the defense insisted, Fuhrman was a racist and a liar.

Bailey introduced the "n-word," *nigger,* into the trial. By working the slur into question after question, he used it to provoke an emotional and unforgiving response from the predominantly black jury. Fuhrman denied having used the hateful word in the previous decade, but Bailey hammered away. Perhaps feeling antagonistic toward the California police for his drunk driving arrest in 1982, Bailey put extra energy behind his abrasive grilling.

At the time, critics said that Bailey botched the Fuhrman cross-examination. They implied he was a has-been. "He didn't seem to have the right style or look for this [jury] . . . it's kind of sad," said Loyola University law professor Laurie Levenson, a frequent commentator on the case. "Mr. Bailey's theatricality and bombast seemed silly at times," commented David Margolick in his coverage for *The New York Times.* "His machismo, most apparent in his constant talk about Mr. Fuhrman's puny flashlight, seemed dated; similarly, his constant, reverent references to the Marines . . . seemed ill suited to a Los Angeles courtroom in 1995."

The last laugh, however, was Bailey's. Months later, defense investigators turned up a would-be screenwriter named Laura Hart McKinny who had conducted hours of interviews with Fuhrman. On her tapes, he called blacks "niggers" 41 times and talked about arresting people without probable cause, destroying or concocting evidence, beating suspects to obtain confessions, and tailoring testimony. Jurors did not hear the tapes but heard McKinny and other witnesses testify about them.

Caught lying under oath, Fuhrman was brought back to the stand, although out of the jury's presence. Not surprisingly, he "took the Fifth Amendment," or

> ❦ "As the wheels of justice grind on, innocence becomes progressively less relevant."

invoked his constitutional right to remain silent and avoid self-incrimination. Under orders from a higher court, jurors were told nothing of this latest development. Instead of resting their case then, as they planned, the defense angrily launched into a new round of testimony concerning DNA and Simpson's gloves.

During the furor, the O. J. Simpson case sometimes seemed like the Mark Fuhrman case, part of the defense strategy all along. Had people lost sight of the trial's focus? Among viewers surveyed by Cable News Network, which had a 700 percent increase in ratings during the trial, only a small number brought up the fact that two people had been killed, or that two young children had lost their mother.

The announcement of the verdict on October 3, 1995, was the most watched 15 minutes in television history. About 150 million Americans saw Simpson—flanked by Johnnie Cochran on his left and F. Lee Bailey on his right—break into a smile as he heard the words "not guilty." After a nine–month trial, the jury reached this decision in barely four hours.

Was O. J. Simpson acquitted because he was black? Rich? Famous? Well-represented? Innocent? *The New York Times* summarized the case as a "national Rorshach test laden with sex, celebrity, wealth, violence, and perhaps most sensitively, race." Public opinion was deeply, painfully divided.

One point was clear. The defense's emphasis on police incompetence and racism was, as Tony Mauro of *USA Today* said, "a ploy that apparently resonated with the mainly black jury." The lawyer who dealt the first "race card" was F. Lee Bailey. "I was critical of Bailey's cross-examination, but . . . in hindsight I see how good he was at entrapping Fuhrman," admitted author Dominick Dunne, who attended the trial daily. "Fuhrman was the trial," wrote the forewoman of the Simpson jury, Armanda Cooley, in her book *Madam Foreman*.

Bailey no longer speaks to Robert Shapiro, the lawyer who recruited him for the Simpson case. The former friends parted ways over the use of racial provocation as a defense strategy. Otherwise, however, the proceedings made Bailey happy and proud to be a trial lawyer. "The presumption of innocence combined with proof beyond a reasonable doubt is what our system has always been about," he concluded.

In January 1996, in civil lawsuits filed by the families of the murdered Nicole Brown Simpson and Ronald Goldman, O. J. Simpson did have to testify under oath about his whereabouts the night of the murders. Though Bailey did not appear at the deposition, he was reported to have helped Simpson prepare for it.

Soon Bailey was making new headlines of his own. In March 1996, he was sentenced to six months in federal prison on charges of civil contempt. Bailey had failed to comply with a judge's order to produce more than $16 million in stocks that he had held in escrow for a former client, the indicted drug trafficker Claude L. Duboc, who had agreed to forfeit those assets to the U.S. government. Bailey spent 44 days in prison, then was freed after surrendering the stocks and also giving up his yacht to the government.

Chronology

June 10, 1933	Francis Lee Bailey born in Waltham, Massachusetts
1950–52	attends Harvard College
1952–57	serves in U.S. Navy and U.S. Marine Corps; marries and has two sons
1957	enters Boston University Law School; opens private detective agency
1960	receives LL.B.; is admitted to the Massachusetts Bar; opens private law practice
1961–69	gains fame as criminal defense lawyer in several murder cases (Sam Sheppard, 1966; Carl Coppolino, 1966–67; "The Boston Strangler," 1967); remarries and has third son
1971–79	defends Captain Ernest Medina in My Lai massacre case (1971); is indicted for mail fraud with ex-client Glenn W. Turner; defends newspaper heiress Patricia Hearst in bank robbery case (1976); writes or co-authors several books on law
1980–present	continues active practice
1994–95	is a member of O. J. Simpson's criminal defense team
1996	sent to federal prison on charges of civil contempt

Further Reading

Bailey, F. Lee with Harvey Aronson. *The Defense Never Rests.* New York: Stein & Day, 1971. Bailey's inside view of the Sheppard and "Boston Strangler" cases, among others, made this book a best–seller.

Bailey, F. Lee with John Greenya. *For the Defense.* New York: Atheneum, 1975. Bailey describes more of his life and work, with extensive coverage of the Medina case.

Davis, Robert. "Legal Legend Steps Into 'Case of the Century.'" *USA Today,* January 4, 1995. An interview with Bailey on the eve of the O. J. Simpson trial.

Frank, Gerald. *The Boston Strangler.* New York: New American Library, 1966. Fascinating account of this gruesome case.

Hearst, Patricia Campbell with Alvin Moscow. *Every Secret Thing.* Garden City, N.Y.: Doubleday & Co., 1982. Patty Hearst's own account of her kidnapping and trial. Critical of Bailey's work.

Locker, Frances C., editor. "F(rancis) Lee Bailey." In *Contemporary Authors,* Volumes 89–92. Detroit: Gale Research, 1980. A short biography, with many good quotes.

Margolick, David. "A Cross-Examination Ends, and Judging Begins, for Simpson Lawyer." *The New York Times,* March 19, 1995. Early commentary on Bailey's role in the Simpson case.

Sarah Weddington
(1945–)

Sarah Weddington, a minister's daughter, initiated and argued the case that legalized abortion in the United States.
(Steve Satterwhite, courtesy of Sarah Weddington)

Roe v. Wade, which legalized abortion, is among the most famous cases decided by the Supreme Court. Surely it is among the most controversial. No one is more surprised by the shock waves of *Roe* than Sarah Ragle Weddington, the lawyer who first argued the case when she was just 25 years old.

Amazingly, *Roe* is Weddington's only major case. In fact, her career has been unlike most others profiled in this book. Weddington will never run for president like Belva Lockwood or John W. Davis, nor be appointed a Supreme Court justice like Robert Jackson or Thurgood Marshall. Yet it is fair to say her work has had as much impact on American life as theirs; some might say it has had more.

The story of Weddington and *Roe v. Wade* reveals many things: how federal courts work, how powerful the Supreme Court is, and how one person made history by, as she says, "putting one legal foot in front of the other."

Sarah Ragle was born on February 5, 1945, in Abilene, Texas. Her father, Herbert, was a Methodist minister who "didn't preach fire-and-brimstone, but the gospel of Christian social concern." Her mother, Lena, was a teacher.

The Methodist Church routinely relocates its ministers, so Sarah grew up in several Texas towns. The experience made her a diplomat: "As a preacher's kid you had to get along with everyone, and I found I could get more done that way."

Outwardly ladylike, Sarah felt stirrings of rebellion in high school but didn't act on them. "I loved basketball but hated the old girls' rules that kept us from running full court," Weddington said in an interview for this book. "But it never occurred to me then to try to change them."

At McMurry College in Abilene, Texas, Sarah studied literature and speech. The dean tried to steer her toward a teaching career. With his own son finding law school hard, he said, surely it would be too tough for a young woman. "That was when I decided I *was* going," Sarah recalls.

At age 20, Sarah entered the University of Texas Law School in

> "My mother would have enjoyed doing the things I did—going to law school, working in government. She pushed me to do what she couldn't."

Austin. She was one of five women among 120 entrants in her class, a ratio that had barely improved since Belva Lockwood studied law almost 100 years earlier. At least men and women no longer had to sit in separate classrooms. Sarah's parents had to put her younger brother and sister through college, so she paid her own law school tuition by working as a clerk-typist in state government. Still she sped through her courses in two years—with one significant interruption.

In 1967 Sarah became pregnant by Ron Weddington, an army veteran and pre-law student whom she married the following year. Unready to start a family, the couple wanted an abortion; however, the procedure was illegal in Texas, except to save the life of the mother. A few other states had slightly less restrictive laws, but nowhere in the United States was abortion legal. Ron got the name of a clinic in Mexico. Abortion was a crime in that country, too, but doctors kept the police away with bribes.

The Mexican clinic charged $400—Sarah's life savings—but the procedure was safe and without complications. That was not often the case. Since the criminalization of abortion in the United States in the mid-1800s, countless women had died from botched procedures or from trying to self-abort using coat hangers or lye.

Although the subject soon became central to Weddington's life, she kept her own abortion secret for 25 years. Why? "There's a lot in our lives we don't go around telling people," she explained recently. "It can be helpful to talk openly about our experiences, but I don't agree with those who say we *must*. Part of why we fought so hard for *Roe* was so women could make such decisions in private."

Weddington's awareness of women's issues was roused by another situation: sexism in the 1960s job market. She was a smart lawyer and a team player, yet law firm after law firm rejected her. It hurt. She recalls: "My male friends who interviewed with the same firms told me they said, 'Sarah was really good and if she just hadn't been a woman we would have snapped her up.'" If a firm had given Weddington a chance, *Roe* historian Marian Faux has speculated, her "feminist side might never have developed so fully."

Weddington needed money, so she took a job researching the document that became the American Bar Association's Code of Professional Responsibility. The project was important, but she was capable of more.

Weddington got involved with a birth control and abortion referral service at the University of Texas. Some volunteers asked her if they could be seen as accomplices to crime, simply for providing information about abortion. To find out, Weddington began researching abortion law.

Around this time, the university banned the on-campus sale of a popular underground newspaper called *The Rag*. That brought an uproar and a lawsuit, which Ron Weddington, now a law student, helped construct. To everyone's astonishment, the case leapfrogged on a technicality to the Supreme Court. That is where the seeds of *Roe v. Wade* germinated. In Sarah Weddington's lawyerly phrase: "The federal court system [seemed to us] a possible route for achieving justice" in abortion rights.

Weddington then knew little about federal courts. She found an informed ally in her law school classmate Linda Coffee, who had clerked in a federal court. The two women decided to build a test case. The first step was to find a plaintiff with standing, the legal term for someone who has a genuine case.

The trail led to Norma McCorvey, alias Jane Roe. After a troubled girlhood, marked by reform schools and suicide attempts, McCorvey married at 16. By 19, she had given up two children for adoption. Pregnant again at 21, with no work experience beyond bartending and selling carnival tickets, McCorvey wanted an abortion, but Texas law made abortion illegal except to save the life of the mother.

At their first meeting, according to Weddington, McCorvey asked if she could obtain an abortion if she said she had been raped. The lawyers told her that Texas law made no such exception. McCorvey went on to say she *was* raped; in 1987, she publicly acknowledged fabricating the rape. When abortion opponents threatened to "expose" and reverse the *Roe* decision, believing it applied only to supposed rape victims like McCorvey, Weddington calmly directed them to original filings, none of which mention the circumstances of Roe's pregnancy. As Weddington has written of McCorvey: " . . . we weren't sure of the real story and our goal was broader than helping victims of rape."

Weddington and Coffee informed McCorvey that any changes in abortion law would come too late for "Jane Roe." McCorvey gave birth to her third child and placed her into adoption before any legal decision was reached. That child, now a mother herself, is an abortion opponent. So is McCorvey, who supported abortion rights for years, but changed her mind in 1995.

To ensure that the case wouldn't be dismissed if its central figure was no longer pregnant, the lawyers filed it as a class-action suit. In *Roe v. Wade,* "Jane Roe" was seeking the right to abortion on behalf of an entire class of people: all pregnant women, now and in the future.

As another backup, Weddington and Coffee prepared a related case: *Doe v. Wade.* The "Wade" both cases opposed was Henry Wade, the district attorney and chief law enforcement official of Dallas County. The "Does" were a Dallas couple who wanted access to legal abortion if their contraceptives failed. For complex medical reasons, Mary Doe had been ordered by her doctor not to get pregnant.

The lawyers had Roe and the Does sign one-page affidavits attesting to their situations. Their participation technically ended there; they never had to risk their anonymity by appearing in any court.

Weddington and Coffee prepared three pages of petitions, claiming that the anti-abortion statutes of Texas denied several rights implied by the U.S. Constitution, including rights to both liberty and privacy. A separate affidavit, by a physician, noted that Texas had originally outlawed abortion in 1854 to protect women against a medically risky procedure—an outmoded reason given the modern availability of safe and antiseptic surgical methods.

In March 1970, Weddington and Coffee paid $30 of their own money to file *Roe* and *Doe*. Before the cases got on the docket, the lawyers filed a last-minute challenge on behalf of James Hallford, M.D. Like most Texas physicians arrested as abortion providers, Hallford was pleading the Fourteenth Amendment. The "due process" clause of this amendment requires laws be clearly written. Doctors argued that Texas laws were vague, and thus unconstitutional, because they did not define which abortion-related situations were "life-threatening."

The court combined the three suits into one. For the lawyers, that was great news: they felt that having a doctor, a single woman, and a married couple as plaintiffs covered all situations.

And so at the age of 25, after a year of groundwork, Weddington argued her first contested case. Sympathetic law professors coached her and Coffee on the fine points of procedure.

The hearing, held in Fifth Circuit Court in Dallas before three judges and no jury, had a rocky start. Defense attorney Jay Floyd, Wade's assistant, immediately moved for dismissal, because Roe might no longer be pregnant, and Mary Doe had never been. The judges denied the request. One judge dryly noted that some students in school desegregation cases were in college by the time their cases were tried.

The tightly timed hearing was not a romp. Coffee had just 13 minutes to argue the technicalities. Because our legal system relies heavily on precedent, or previous cases, she concentrated on these earlier cases.

Two then-recent cases, *People of California v. Belous* and *U.S. v.*

> ❦ "If someone had told me in 1973 that I would still be working to save the legality of abortion today, I wouldn't have believed it."

125

Vuitch (based in Washington, D.C.), had found state abortion laws to be vague, and in violation of basic rights to personal liberty. Coffee reminded the judges that *Belous* also put women's rights ahead of the state's interest in protecting the unborn. Most important, Coffee cited a famous 1961 Supreme Court case, *Griswold v. Connecticut*, which struck down an antiquated state law that had forbidden the sale of contraceptives even to married couples. *Griswold* was crucial because it said individuals have a "zone of privacy" in which to make personal choices, implied, although not specified, by the First and Fourteenth Amendments.

Weddington's arguments were less technical. When asked if legalized abortion would promote promiscuity, she answered that many young women were already sexually active and "those unable to shoulder the responsibility of a child . . . should be entitled to an abortion." Throughout her argument, she emphasized that the choice should belong to the woman—not to the state, or even to the physician.

Soon the court declared Texas's anti-abortion laws to be vague and unconstitutional. Victory? Not quite, because the judges would not issue an order to block District Attorney Wade from enforcing the old laws. In legal terms, the gap between declaration and action is the difference between "declarative relief" and "injunctive relief."

Wade told the press he would continue prosecuting doctors who performed abortions. Under a procedural quirk, Wade's announcement paved the way for Weddington and Coffee to bypass all intermediate appeals. Shades of *The Rag* situation! The women quickly petitioned the U.S. Supreme Court to hear *Roe.*

The Supreme Court accepts 100 to 180 cases among the more than 5,000 it is asked to review each year. The Court decides another 100 to 200 cases by written opinion only, without oral arguments. The nine justices vote on which cases to accept. If four vote yes, the case is heard.

Why was *Roe* chosen, especially when it turned out to be only one of twelve abortion rights cases up for top court review that year? The time was right. Abortion had so entangled the lower courts that the Supreme Court had to step in. Weddington thinks *Roe* made the cut, along with a Georgia case called *Doe v. Bolton,* because the cases represented a spectrum: Texas' abortion laws were strict, while Georgia's were less so. "Lenient" laws, in those days, often required women to establish residency, gain approval from a medical board, and meet other requirements before obtaining an abortion.

Preparing a Supreme Court case is demanding, even for the experienced lawyer. Months in advance, the Court wants a full record of all earlier proceedings; supplemental appendices of relevant legal, medical, and sociological information; and a lengthy brief setting out closely reasoned legal arguments for the case. In addition, lawyers usually solicit *amici curiae,* or "friends of the court" briefs, to bolster their arguments. All materials must be submitted according to strict formats and short deadlines.

These requirements can keep a huge law firm busy for months. They are also costly; one estimate put *Roe*'s minimal budget at $69,000. Yet Weddington handled much of the preparation and fund-raising herself. She had to quit her new job as city attorney for Fort Worth to do it. Coffee and Ron Weddington helped as their jobs allowed.

Attorneys at the James Madison Law Institute in New York City, an abortion rights advocacy center, agreed to prepare the brief. That eased Weddington's burden—until she realized that the Institute was disorganized, and the all-important document was not being written. She and Ron spent a frenzied summer in New York picking up the pieces.

They managed to gather, file, and publicize 40 *amicus* briefs by August—impressive statements of support from "friends" such as state attorneys general; the American College of Obstetricians and Gynecologists; and several religious bodies, including the United Methodist Church, Sarah's father's denomination. Four opponents filed "non-friend" statements. Crucially, the main brief reached the Supreme

The Supreme Court justices who ultimately ruled on Roe v. Wade. *Front: Potter Stewart; William O. Douglas; Chief Justice Warren E. Burger; William J. Brennan, Jr.; Byron R. White. Back: Lewis F. Powell, Jr.; Thurgood Marshall; Harry A. Blackmun (who wrote the majority opinion); William H. Rehnquist.*
(Photo by Harris & Ewing, Collection of the Supreme Court of the United States)

Court in time. The Weddingtons then returned to Austin for weeks of moot court rehearsals, in which law students and professors vied for the chance to play "the Supremes"—their pet name for Supreme Court justices.

Entering the Supreme Court on December 13, 1971, to argue *Jane Roe et al. Appellant v. Henry Wade,* Weddington "felt a calm produced by months of preparation." The hushed chambers with their velvet curtains reminded her of a church, which added to her comfort. Ron and her mother were there to silently cheer her on. Coffee took part, but Weddington handled the oral argument. She had 30 minutes to make her case, and opted to save five minutes for rebuttal.

The approach to *Roe* in the Supreme Court was much like the approach in Texas. Weddington again argued that the original basis for criminalizing abortion—to protect women from medical risk—was no longer valid. She offered facts to prove that Texas did not treat fetuses as persons: the state did not prosecute the murder of a pregnant woman as a double homicide; property rights were contingent on being born. Weddington expanded this argument to a federal level. The Fourteenth Amendment, she noted, referred to citizens as "all persons born or naturalized" in the United States. She spoke plainly: "The Constitution, as I read it . . . attaches protection to the person at the time of birth. Those persons *born* are citizens."

The opposing side repeated most of its Texas arguments as well. Jay Floyd began: "It's an old joke, but when a man argues against two beautiful ladies like this, they're going to have the last word." No one laughed.

Floyd argued, futilely, that Jane Roe couldn't represent pregnant women since by now she had surely given birth. He claimed that the fetus does have legal rights, which the state has an interest in protecting. The justices asked him why abortion providers in Texas were not charged with premeditated murder, but rather the lesser charge of felony murder. In a long exchange that did end in laughter—nervous laughter from spectators—Floyd could not answer Justice Thurgood Marshall's question about when life began according to Texas law. "I don't—Mr. Justice—there are unanswerable questions in this field," he stammered.

In an hour, the session was over. Weddington felt frustrated: "I tried to return to the points I knew I had to make and win, but the justices kept interrupting." That afternoon, the Court would hear *Doe v. Bolton.* Then there would be nothing to do but wait.

Supreme Court decisions take time. The justices do additional research, confer, hold a vote, and write their opinions. They issue their decisions by late June, before recessing until October. But something very unusual happened with *Roe* and *Doe*. On June 26, 1972, the Court officially postponed both cases for reargument. Why? Rumors abounded.

There were two vacancies on the Court in December 1971, so only seven justices heard the abortion cases argued. That was enough for a legal ruling, but the Court may have wanted its full membership to make this landmark decision. Another theory is that Richard Nixon, running for his second term as president, pressured the Court to postpone the ruling so as not to disrupt his campaign. *Roe* historians believe that Justice Harry Blackmun, the Court's specialist on medical issues, wanted more time for research.

"I did not know what I could say during a second presentation that would be more persuasive than the earlier arguments," Weddington reflected. Back home she was busy campaigning for a seat in the Texas House of Representatives. When she won, one of her first moves was to prepare a new state law on abortion rights in case *Roe* was lost.

Weddington did new work on *Roe*. She wrote an updated brief, noting that the American Bar Association was calling for a Unified Abortion Rights Act. She added that hundreds of Texas women were traveling to New York for abortions, where the procedure had recently been fully legalized. In moot courts, she tried to polish her delivery.

On October 11, 1972, both sides returned to the Supreme Court. "This time there was no electricity to the hearing," Weddington said. Interruptions by the justices, which had so distracted her the first time around, were eerily absent.

Questions about the fetus took precedence. Justice Byron White asked Weddington: "Would you lose your case if [we held that] the fetus was a person?" "Then you would have a balancing of interests," she answered. That concept arose again, when defense attorney Robert Flowers conceded that Texas law put women first in balancing the interests of the woman and the fetus in life-threatening situations.

Justice Potter Stewart questioned Flowers about his claim that life begins at conception. "Now how should that question be decided? Is it a legal question, a constitutional question, a medical question . . . what is it?" he demanded. Blackmun observed that the medical profession could not agree on the issue, and Flowers had to concur.

> ❦ "**F**or me, abortion is symbolic of who gets to make the decision. For opponents, I think it's symbolic of everything they oppose in recent years."

Weddington went home feeling that *Roe* had a chance. She was distracted by a growing rift with Ron. "We were both lawyers, but I was known for arguing a Supreme Court case," she has explained. "We had both run for political office, but I had won." They divorced amicably in 1974.

The Court's 7–2 decision in favor of *Roe*, announced on January 22, 1973, overturned anti-abortion laws in 46 states. The Court also decided in favor of *Doe*, remembered as the case that allows abortions to be done outside hospitals, as long as providers are licensed physicians. Weddington rejoiced, although her official statement was characteristically low-key:

> *I am pleased because of the impact this decision will have on the lives of many women who in the past have suffered because of the current Texas law. I am especially pleased that the decision is a solid 7 to 2 decision and that it was based on the right to privacy. I feel very humble to be able to represent the class of women affected by this decision and hope their lives will be better for it.*

Blackmun, a lifelong Republican, wrote the majority opinion. This opinion agrees that restrictive abortion laws were outdated; claims that under the Fourteenth and Ninth Amendments, women have a right to privacy, including the right to decide whether or not to have children; and states that the word "person" in the Constitution lacks "any possible prenatal application."

At the same time, the Court gave the states leeway to regulate, for the protection of the woman, how abortions are

Demonstrators gather yearly in Washington, D.C., on January 22, the anniversary of the Supreme Court's decision to legalize abortion.
(LCU9-35666A-11, U.S. News and World Report Collection, Library of Congress)

performed. What surprised all observers about Blackmun's opinion was that he provided a strict trimester formula— something that had never come up in the courtroom.

A separate document spelled out the trimester guidelines. It allows abortion without interference in the first three months of pregnancy. In that period, the state can only insist that a woman consult with a physician. These restrictions only protect the woman's health in months four through six; and makes abortion illegal after six months, unless the woman's life or health are in danger. Six months is the point at which many medical experts say the fetus is capable of living outside the womb. Fewer than one in ten thousand U.S. abortions take place that late.

There were two strong dissenting opinions. Justice William Rehnquist wrote: "An operation such as [abortion] is not 'private' in the ordinary usage of the word." In vehement language, Justice Byron White said the majority opinion twisted the meaning of the Constitution to value "the convenience, whim, or caprice of the putative mother more than the life or potential life of the fetus."

It is not possible within the scope of this profile to describe the subsequent effects of *Roe*. The decision triggered a battle—aptly called "a clash of absolutes"—that over the years has escalated in violence, including bombings and murders.

Apart from its many other effects, *Roe* has shown the American public that the Supreme Court's judgments are indeed "supreme;" lower courts cannot override them without constitutional challenges. *Roe* could be struck down by passage of a new constitutional amendment, one that defines the start of life at conception, but this process is difficult and rarely attempted. The Supreme Court could issue a superseding decision. This doesn't happen often—the Court has reversed fewer than 200 of its tens of thousands of decisions since 1789.

However, subsequent Supreme Court decisions have amplified *Roe*, sometimes expanding it, and often narrowing it. These are the chief examples.

Planned Parenthood of Missouri v. Danforth (1976) struck down parental consent laws, and also held that a husband does not have the power to deny his wife an abortion. *Beal v. Doe and Maher v. Doe (1977)* ruled that states are not required to spend Medicaid funds on elective abortions. *Bellotti v. Baird* (1979) allowed states to require parental consent for minors seeking abortions, as long as an alternative process, such as a judge's consent, was offered. *Harris v. MacRae* (1980) denied government payment for any abortions for women on welfare. *Webster v. Reproductive Health Care* (1989) granted states new authority to curb abortions in tax-supported institutions. *Rust v. Sullivan* (1991) ushered in the so-called gag rule that denies government aid to family

> ❦ "There are so many things I wanted to do but I'm seen as too controversial."

planning clinics that provide abortion information.

The strongest threat to the *Roe v. Wade* decision, has been *Planned Parenthood of Southeastern Pennsylvania v. Casey* (1992). This decision upheld many of Pennsylvania's requirements, including a mandatory 24-hour waiting period, "informed consent" about the facts of fetal development, and parental or judicial consent for minors. *Casey* stopped short of overturning *Roe.* The Supreme Court is expected to rule on a challenge to a 1994 Federal law, the Freedom of Access to Clinic Entrances Act, which currently makes it a crime to block entry to abortion clinics.

Roe has shaped Weddington's professional life. It put her once-bright political career into limbo. In addition to holding state office, she enjoyed what she describes as a "fabulous" few years as special assistant to President Jimmy Carter, helping to expand opportunities for women in the military and obtaining the first funding to help victims of domestic violence. In 1992, journalist Leslie Bennetts called her "a living footnote" whose opportunities have been "eternally blighted by the very breakthrough that made her famous."

Weddington continues to keep a law office in Austin. She teaches pre-law classes on leadership and gender equity at the University of Texas, and lectures and writes frequently on leadership issues, as well as abortion rights.

Anger and bitterness are not part of Weddington's style. Even in debates with Phyllis Schafly and other arch-opponents of abortion, even when faced with pickets and threats, she remains soft-spoken and composed.

What is the source of her calm? "Part of it is my legal training, which stresses reason over anger, at least in public," she says. "But mainly I want to keep people listening to what I say—to the *substance* of it. The higher the volume that people use—the more angry, condemning, and belligerent they sound—the less they're listened to."

Like Belva Lockwood and Clarence Darrow, Weddington has become a star on the lecture circuit. She is popular among college students, who have never known a time when abortion was illegal. Her message seeks common ground: "The battle was never 'for abortion'—abortion was not what we wanted to encourage. The battle was for the basic right of women to make their own decisions. That is the underlying question: Who is to control and define the lives of women?"

Chronology

Further Reading and Viewing

Bennetts, Leslie. "A Woman's Choice." *Vanity Fair,* September 1992. A short profile of Weddington that is revealing and sometimes critical.

Bonavoglia, Angela. *The Choices We Made: 25 Women & Men Speak Out About Abortion.* New York: Random House, 1991. Contains a chapter by the real "Jane Roe," Norma McCorvey, who never had an abortion.

Caruana, Claudia. *The Abortion Debate.* Brookfield, Conn.: The Millbrook Press, 1992. An excellent overview for young readers: short, balanced, packed with information and good photos.

Cozic, Charles P. and Jonathan Petrikin, editors. *The Abortion Controversy.* San Diego, Calif.: Greenhaven Press, 1995. A collection of essays in which people on both sides of the debate discuss the morality and legality of abortion. Contains a wealth of suggested readings, as well as an extensive directory of pro-choice and anti-abortion organizations.

Faux, Marian. *Roe v. Wade: The Untold Story of the Landmark Supreme Court Decision That Made Abortion Legal.* New York: Macmillan, 1988. Highly detailed; factual yet dramatic.

Roe v. Wade. A made-for-television movie based on the case. Scenes about the legal aspects are generally accurate, according to Weddington. First broadcast by NBC in 1989.

Weddington, Sarah. *A Question of Choice.* New York: Grosset/Putnam, 1992. Partly autobiographical, but mainly a history of Weddington's involvement in *Roe* and in subsequent pro-choice activities.

Linda Fairstein
(1947–)

Linda Fairstein is an expert on rape prosecution. Above her desk is a photo of President John F. Kennedy, one of her teenage heroes, who helped inspire her to pursue a career in public service.
(Marian Calabro)

---

*N*ick and Cindy, college friends, are on their first date. Within a few hours, Cindy will accuse Nick of rape. Nick will say they had sex because Cindy asked for it.

How will the police treat Cindy when she reports the rape? If this case goes to trial, whom will the jury believe?

Cindy, a real person, is one of the thousands of women defended by Linda Fairstein, the leading expert on prosecuting sex crimes. In a rough arena, Fairstein is polished, always poised, and in command of her facts. She dresses elegantly in fine suits and high heels that add stature to her tall frame. She listens intently and patiently; crime victims, women and men alike, find her easy to talk to and trust, and are relieved to have her on their side.

Some of Fairstein's courtroom battles, like the one involving "preppy murderer" Robert Chambers, inspired books and movies. Other cases made headlines: sexual assaults by a homeless man against a homeless woman, by a Boy Scout leader against his charges, by a dentist or gynecologist against a patient. Whether a case is sensational or sadly routine, Fairstein and her staff have the same goals for each one, to convict guilty assailants and to bring survivors through the criminal justice system with dignity and hope.

Linda Fairstein was born in 1947 in Mount Vernon, New York, a suburb of New York City; her childhood was comfortable and unremarkable. A stable background, she believes, helps her withstand the pressures of her job. "I'm very lucky," she said in an interview for this book. "My life has been well-adjusted and trauma-free."

Fairstein's father, Samuel, was a doctor; her mother, Alice, a nurse. They didn't steer Linda and her brother, who also became a lawyer, into any particular careers, but they did impart their belief in the importance of helping others. "Life, death, caregiving—that was the stuff of our daily dinner conversations," Fairstein recalls.

"I wouldn't have had the stomach for a medical career," she adds, echoing William Kunstler's feelings. It's a curious statement given the sordidness of many of her cases. She laughs easily when the irony is pointed out.

At Vassar College in Poughkeepsie, New York, Fairstein was an English major. She was drawn to law as an outlet for her talents in research, writing, and reasoning. In 1969 she entered law school at the University of Virginia.

*District Attorney Robert M. Morgenthau chose Fairstein to head
Manhattan's Sex Crimes Prosecution Unit. "Criminal law suits Linda," he
said. "She's got the temperament that can deal with the pressure."*
(District Attorney's Office, New York County)

Criminal law hooked her at once: "I loved its immediacy,
the human problems and resolutions." So instead of consid-
ering a career at a private firm, she set her sights on the

Office of the District Attorney of New York County. The D.A.'s Office adjudicates all reported crimes in Manhattan. For would-be prosecutors, those who long to be up to their necks in every type of crime, it is Mecca.

Fairstein knew that Frank Hogan, the Manhattan district attorney who served from 1943 to 1976, did not generally encourage women lawyers. During her final year of law school, she applied to work for him anyway and passed her first round of interviews. A few months later, Hogan summoned her to his office. Fairstein paraphrases what he told her.

"I look at you," Hogan said, "and I see a young woman from a good family, educated at the best schools, with absolutely nothing in your background to prepare you for what you would be exposed to in a place like this. It's tawdry, Miss Fairstein, it's very tawdry. Frankly, I have to tell you I think this is no place for a woman like you."

Fairstein was accustomed to working hard and getting what she wanted. She felt dejected and wasn't sure what to do next. A few weeks later, Hogan called. Did Fairstein still want the "tawdry" job? She certainly did.

Of the 160 assistant D.A.s on staff when Fairstein began there in fall 1972, only seven were women. By the 1990s the staff had grown to about 300 men and 300 women. Hogan asked incoming assistants to commit to a four-year stay, so they could learn every aspect of public prosecution. Fairstein agreed, despite secret doubts. The issue was not the job itself. "I just knew I would be married and having kids by then," she once told a reporter.

As it turned out, Fairstein remained single for another 15 years. Four years after joining the D.A.'s Office, she not only planned to stay, but was such a star performer that Hogan's successor, Robert M. Morgenthau, asked her to head the Sex Crimes Prosecution Unit. The SCPU is a special division of the D.A.'s Office, created in 1974.

While Fairstein was flattered, she hesitated at accepting. Would the new job be too limiting? Did she have enough

> ❦ "Do not delay in reporting a rape, or any crime. You can never regain the advantage of early reporting."

experience for it? Morgenthau reminded her that she had learned as much as any assistant D.A. about the unique and horrible category of sex crimes.

This was true. During her training, Fairstein had interviewed hundreds of rape victims and participated in a few sex crimes trials. She was good at it. Other prosecutors hungered after high-profile murder cases, and Fairstein was enjoying a stint on a team devoted to prosecuting career criminals. However, she knew an opportunity when she saw one.

To say the job worked out is an understatement; Fairstein and the SCPU have become synonymous. Some 20 years later, she marveled at her initially ambivalent reaction to being offered the job: "The most richly rewarding job, to my view, in law enforcement, and yet my vision was so narrow I had to be prodded to take it!" The unit is so successful at convicting criminals that it has been copied in cities the world over. In any given month, Fairstein and her staff train prosecutors from all over the country, who come to New York at their own expense. Some cities and states are still far behind New York in their handling of sex crimes and victims, but Fairstein says that's changing, "especially as more women come into the criminal justice system as judges and prosecutors."

Fairstein assumed leadership of the SCPU at a pivotal time. Throughout the country, and especially in New York State, laws concerning rape were changing rapidly.

Incredible as it may seem now, until the 1970s it was almost impossible to bring a rape case to trial in the United States. The reasons were embedded in British statutes written in 1671 and carried over to American law.

If the alleged crime was anything but rape, any adult's accusation was sufficient to press charges. However, in the case of rape, the prosecution had to prove three things, *beyond the victim's word:* 1) the identity of the assailant, despite the fact that rape is the least likely crime to be witnessed by a third party; 2) the sexual nature of the attack, traditionally evidenced by the presence of semen, despite the fact that rape can occur without ejaculation, and frantic victims can scrub, swallow, or gag all traces of semen; and 3) "earnest resistance" on the part of the plaintiff, despite the fact that victims who try to resist are often threatened with death at the point of a knife or gun.

For centuries, then, an absurd inequality was embedded in the law. "You were legally competent to testify about a man who held you up at knifepoint and took your wallet," Fairstein interprets, "but if in the same transaction he raped you as well, you were *not* legally competent to testify."

After 300 years, these archaic laws yielded to pressure from victim's rights groups and feminists. Reform occurred state by state throughout the 1970s and 1980s. As they instituted reform, most states also took the huge step of adding rape shield laws. What is shielded is any courtroom discussion of the plaintiff's sexual history. Defendants lost the age-old ploy of putting the plaintiff's personal life, rather than the crime, on trial. In New York and some other states, evidence of prior sexual conduct is sometimes admissible, such as when a previous sexual relationship exists between plaintiff and defendant.

Men, too, can be rape victims, Fairstein notes. Although male-on-male rapes are still "stigmatized and underreported," reformed rape laws protect men as well as women.

Fears of false reports have not been realized; Fairstein estimates "completely false reporting at about 5 percent," on par with other types of crimes. "In perhaps 30 percent of date rape reports, the victim may lie [about some aspect] but is not making the whole thing

> ❦ "**U**se of alcohol and drugs makes the date rape victim more vulnerable. Her ability to respond and recall details is affected."

up," she adds. "What we're here to do is to apply the legal definition. Was a crime committed—a forced act of intercourse?"

The case of Nick and Cindy, mentioned earlier, illustrates some typical features of date rape. The people knew each other and partook of drugs and alcohol before the attack. The woman, however, quickly reported the rape. By contrast, most date rape victims delay reporting for days or weeks, if at all.

Nick and Cindy, both 25, were casual friends and classmates at ballet school. After wine and dinner at a restaurant—their first date—Nick accompanied Cindy back to her apartment and said he wanted her "now." He slapped her when she refused to take off her clothes. Cindy fought and screamed, but Nick grabbed her neck and wrestled her to the floor. He told her he was taking out his anger on a girlfriend who had left him. Nick raped and sodomized Cindy, then fell asleep on her floor.

Cindy fled at 3 A.M. to the home of some friends. Over her fears—"who will believe me?"—they urged her to report the rape. Police officers responded immediately, and returned with Cindy to her home, where Nick was still sleeping. He awoke to an arrest. The police urged Cindy to have a post-rape medical examination, which she did.

When Fairstein interviewed Cindy the next day, she encountered a problem. There was a slight discrepancy in the victim's report to the police. Cindy had been afraid to report that she and Nick had smoked marijuana before dinner. That fact could work against Cindy if Nick mentioned it in court and she didn't.

Coaxing out the victim's full story may not seem like a prosecution tactic, but it is vital. When interviewing victims, Fairstein and her staff gently encourage total honesty. The interviews are usually one-on-one, because victims sometimes omit painful details in the presence of family members. The aim is to build trust between lawyer and client, and eliminate "surprises" in the courtroom.

As Fairstein points out, if the jury discovers "just enough reason to distrust a plaintiff on something minor, their faith in her entire story is undermined." She recalls losing a case because "the jury couldn't believe a defendant was raped and then went to the beach the next day."

The defense strives to plant such mistrust; their most common strategy is to call the plaintiff a liar. Nick's version of the evening was that Cindy had invited him up for sex, loved it, then falsely cried rape on learning he had another girlfriend.

Unlike some acquaintance rape cases, this one had outside corroboration. Two of Cindy's neighbors testified to hearing her scream. Nevertheless, the case ended in a mistrial when one juror held out for Nick's innocence. Mistrials are automatically retried. At a second trial, Nick was found guilty and sent to prison for four to twelve years.

Every day, at least one woman like Cindy, and often as many as five, makes way to the Sex Crimes Prosecution Unit. Headquartered in unglamorous offices at 100 Centre Street in downtown Manhattan, the SCPU gives victims the privacy needed to tell their stories. It removes them from the "conveyor belt" of the D.A.'s office at large, and directs them to medical and psychological counseling as necessary.

"Rape is a crime of sexual violence, which sets it apart from every other kind of criminality," Fairstein emphasizes. The entire SCPU staff—the director, a secretary, up to twenty-five assistant district attorneys, two paralegals, and a full-time police detective—is specially trained in this sensitive area, as is the New York City Police Department investigative unit working closely with the SCPU.

In recent years Fairstein has stepped back from trying cases to devote her time to operations, training, and trial strategy. She oversees some 500 to 700 sex crime cases annually (not all go to trial), and takes pride in the SCPU's high conviction rate, "about 90 percent for stranger rapes and 60 to 65 percent for acquaintance rapes."

Of a typical year's cases, between 100 and 200 are classified as felonies, usually because they involve extreme violence

🦂 "**T**he easiest case I ever had, the man had a scorpion tattooed on his penis. That's not the kind of evidence you get with someone who held up a bank."

and/or career criminality, and are tried in the New York State Supreme Court. Another 100 cases are plea-bargained, meaning that the offender pleads guilty in exchange for no trial and a lighter sentence. Fairstein defends the limited use of plea bargains, citing overcrowded courtrooms and noting that SCPU prosecutors "bargain" away very little jail time. The balance of cases, the majority, are tried before juries of Manhattan citizens.

Most sex crimes that go to trial in urban areas, says Fairstein, are date rapes. Non-acquaintance rapes, or stranger rapes as the SCPU calls them, follow different patterns and are easier to prosecute. Because these crimes reflect the most common public image of rape—a brutal attack by an unknown assailant—jurors are less likely to blame victims. The prosecutor's main concern is to identify the attacker accurately and to make the identification stick.

Sometimes identification is easy, as victims are often forced to study their attackers intimately. The process can be aided by DNA testing, which compares the defendant's semen to any recovered from the crime, Fairstein calls DNA technology "the best news" on the anti-rape scene because "the genetic print left at the crime scene will not change."

However, DNA testing isn't perfect. It can lack accuracy, and is almost useless in gang rapes, where semen samples are mixed. The process is also expensive and less widely used than the media focus might indicate.

When accurate identification is difficult, prosecuting stranger rape can be a nightmare. The assault on the Central Park jogger was one such example. "Just when you think you've seen it all, something else comes along . . . I had never seen a gang rape involving 39 kids," Fairstein told *People Weekly* magazine.

Linda Fairstein

Linda Fairstein and opposing attorney Jack Litman confer with Judge Howard E. Bell during the "preppy murder" trial. Defendant Robert Chambers is sketched at right.
(Marilyn Church)

The jogger, a young banker, was raped in Central Park on April 19, 1989. Numerous assailants who had been out "wilding" beat her into a coma, raped and sodomized her, bound and gagged her, then fled. At 1:30 A.M. two walkers discovered the woman near death. (As with most rape victims, her real name has never been released.)

In the meantime, as other crimes were being committed during the "wilding" spree, the police were making arrests. After finding out about the attack the next day, Fairstein spent 32 hours at the police station where several suspects were being held. She overheard suspect Kharey Wise, age 16, joking about the rape. Just after dawn, Fairstein led police detectives, Wise, and another suspect—14-year-old Kevin

Richardson—to the scene. Dried blood covered the area. She pointed to it. "This is where it happened . . . the raping," Fairstein heard Richardson say.

"Damn. Damn. That's a lotta blood. I knew she was bleeding but I couldn't see how much," Fairstein heard Wise say.

Fairstein, as a witness, testified to these and other comments at a pretrial hearing, helping to strengthen the charges against the five leading suspects. Five other suspects took plea bargains; others were tried as minors in Family Court. Furthermore, Fairstein's actions proved crucial when William Kunstler, co-counsel for suspect Yusef Salaam, argued that the suspect's written and videotaped statements were coerced, and when DNA testing proved inconclusive.

The large number of defendants necessitated two separate trials. Fairstein worked in the background; the courtroom work fell mainly to Senior Assistant District Attorney Elizabeth Lederer, who won an attempted murder conviction for Kevin Richardson. He and the other main suspects were found guilty of rape, assault, riot, and other charges.

Fairstein tried the case against "preppy murderer" Robert Chambers. Her first homicide trial, it called for all of her strengths: investigative savvy, careful preparation, an unruffled demeanor, and sharp intelligence. "If there were more people like her it would be an infinitely juster [legal] system," New York University law professor Burt Neuborne observed after the Chambers case. "She doesn't fight dirty, but she fights hard."

Chambers claimed he accidentally strangled Jennifer Levin, a friend, during "rough sex" in Central Park on August 26, 1986. Chambers's attorney, Jack Litman, presented Levin as a promiscuous woman, and wanted her "sex diary" (actually an address book) placed in evidence. Fairstein fought this fiercely, with success. The media feasted on the debate. In a rape case, the shield law would have automatically ruled out any discussion of Levin's sexual history. As a direct result of the Chambers case, New York State shield laws have been extended to cover homicides with sexual components.

The Chambers case came to trial in 1988, after eight grueling weeks of jury selection. The trial lasted 13 weeks, a record for a single-defendant case in New York County. The following exchange illustrates Fairstein's smart questioning, and ability to think on her feet. She is cross-examining Ronald L. Kornblum, M.D., an expert witness on strangling.

Fairstein: When you used the language 'doing the chicken,' would you describe for us exactly what phenomenon you described?

Kornblum: That's a term police used on the West Coast for someone who has had the carotid choke applied to him and he develops seizures [and] various other uncommon maneuvers.

Fairstein: Well, do you specifically describe these uncommon maneuvers as victims grimacing with pain, flailing the arms and legs, victims going into convulsions? Is that correct?

Kornblum: Yes.

Fairstein used Chambers's own expert witness to raise doubt about the young man's contention that Levin died instantly, while his hands were around her neck. In her final summation, four hours long, Fairstein spoke eloquently of Levin's painful and far-from-instantaneous death.

Opposing attorney Jack Litman also scored his points. Levin spent her last night alive partying at a bar with friends. He cross-examined several of them so skillfully that one actually said Jennifer regarded Robert as "a piece of meat." In her book on the case, *Wasted,* journalist Linda Wolfe wrote that Litman didn't need any sex diary "to attack Jennifer Levin— her girlfriends did it for her."

After nine days of deliberation, the jury seemed deadlocked. Overwrought jurors begged the judge to be excused. Foreseeing a mistrial, Fairstein and Litman agreed to a plea bargain. Chambers pleaded guilty to a lesser charge— manslaughter, not premeditated murder—and was sentenced to five to fifteen years, not eight and one-third to twenty-five

> ❦ "Rapists come in every shape, size, and background."

years. His subsequent requests for parole have been denied, due largely to petitions circulated by Jennifer Levin's mother, now a crusader for victims' rights.

Some critics accused Fairstein of caving in, but she defends the plea bargain as realistic. "For someone to spend the years from [age] 21 to 31 incarcerated is no small victory," she told *Ms.* magazine. She also noted that Levin's family was satisfied with the sentence. When asked why the jury could not reach a consensus, Fairstein speculated it was because "jurors are still influenced by class and race."

Appearances in general sway juries, Fairstein added. She finds that women, especially, may overlook evidence against defendants who are attractive and articulate. "He couldn't have done it; he doesn't *look* like a rapist," they sometimes say. This exasperates Fairstein, who once said she would prefer all-male juries in date rape cases.

Many commentators seized on the Central Park jogger case as a symbol of racial polarity—the assailants were black, the jogger white—and the Chambers case as an example of arrogance among the young and rich. Fairstein sees rape as a crime, not a metaphor; she rejects "rape" as a blanket term for oppression against women. People who use the phrase "date rape" to describe sexual harassment will quickly be corrected: "That minimizes the traumatic nature of a forced act of intercourse and does a terrible disservice to rape survivors," she insists.

After two decades of directing the SCPU, Fairstein still finds her work immensely rewarding. Family, friends, and office staff, she says, help her avoid burnout. Her duties in the D.A.'s Office have expanded—she is also deputy chief of the Trial Division—and her name has been raised as a future Manhattan district attorney or U.S. attorney general.

In the meantime, the English major has reemerged. Fairstein's husband, attorney Justin Feldman, once joked that she should write the kind of detective mysteries she loves to read. In 1995 she signed a $500,000 contract to write two such books. Her fictional prosecutor "has some of my traits but is younger, thinner, and blonder than I am."

Linda Fairstein will never stray far from her roots as a prosecutor. "My most gratifying cases aren't necessarily those that wind up in the newspapers," she summarizes. "They're the ones where the victim expects little from the system and says 'but it's just my word against his.' Not only can I tell her that's all the law requires now, but very often we can take the case to trial and get her rapist convicted."

Chronology

▬▬▬▬▬

May 5, 1947	Linda Fairstein born in Mount Vernon, New York
1969	graduates from Vassar College
1972	graduates from law school at the University of Virginia; joins the Office of the District Attorney of New York County, one of seven women on 160-person staff
1973	gains experience in various areas of the D.A.'s Office; prosecutes first rape case
1976	chosen to head New York County's Sex Crimes Prosecution Unit (SCPU)
1976–present	continues as Assistant District Attorney and Director of the SCPU, overseeing its operations and growth
1987	marries Justin N. Feldman
1988	prosecutes the Robert Chambers "Preppy Murder" case
1989–90	oversees prosecution strategy for trials involving the gang rape of a jogger in Central Park

Further Reading

Bouton, Katherine. "Linda Fairstein vs. Rape." *The New York Times Magazine,* February 25, 1990. Outlines Fairstein's career and gives a good sense of her life on the job.

Couric, Emily. *The Trial Lawyers: The Nation's Top Litigators Tell How They Win.* New York: St. Martin's Press, 1988. The chapter on Fairstein, the only woman profiled in the book, contains good background information.

DiMona, Lisa and Constance Herndon, editors. *The 1995 Information Please Women's Sourcebook.* Boston: Houghton Mifflin, 1994. Part fact book, part directory, it has an excellent section on rape, violence, and women's safety.

Fairstein, Linda A. *Sexual Violence: Our War Against Rape.* New York: William Morrow & Company, Inc., 1993. Fairstein focuses on the workings of New York's Sex Crimes Prosecution Unit, and on her career development. Though she grippingly traces a serial rape case from beginning to end, she barely discusses more famous trials, like that of Robert Chambers.

Reed, Susan. "Linda Fairstein: A Sex Crimes Prosecutor Bolsters Her Case—and Her Name—by Being Tough and Tender." *People,* September 27, 1993. Personal and professional profile.

Sullivan, Tim. *Unequal Verdicts: The Central Park Jogger Trials.* New York: American Lawyer Books/Simon and Schuster, 1992. A lawyer/journalist delves into the Central Park jogger case.

Wolfe, Linda. *Wasted: The Preppie Murder.* New York: Simon and Schuster, 1989. The in-depth book on the Robert Chambers case.

Index

Boldface numbers indicate main topics.
Italic page numbers indicate illustrations or captions.
Page numbers followed by *c* indicate chronology.

155

Index

157

Index

radicalization of, 85–86, 89, 94

L

labor law
  Darrow's cases, 18, 21–23, 24, 32
  Davis's cases, 36, 37
land claims, Native American, 10–13, 15, 95
landmark cases, 73–74, 130; *See also Brown vs. Board of Education of Topeka*; *Roe v. Wade*
Law School Admission Council, xii
law schools, women students, xi–xii, 4–5, 122
lecture circuit
  Darrow's appearances, 25
  Lockwood's tours, *8*, 10
  Weddington's appearances, 135, 136
Lederer, Elizabeth, 148
Legal Aid Society, x
Leopold, Nathan, Jr., viii, 25–27, 32
Levenson, Laurie, 115
Levin, Jennifer, 148, 149, 150
Levin, Meyer, 27
lie detectors, ix, 104–5, *108*
Lincoln University, 70, 76, 82
literacy tests, 77
litigation explosion, xi
Litman, Jack, *147*, 148, 149
Little Rock (Arkansas), school desegregation, 75
Lockwood, Belva, *1*, **1–16**
  background, 2–3, 52
  career as educator, 3–4, 14
  chronology, 14c–15c
  first legal cases, 5–6
  honors, 13
  lecture fees and tours, *8*, 10
  legal practice in federal courts, 7
  Native American land claims case, 10–13, 95
  U.S. presidential candidacy, 9–10, 15
Lockwood, Ezekiel, 4, 14
Lockwood, Jessie, 4, 14
Loeb, Richard, viii, 25–27, 32
Los Angeles Times bombing case (1911), 24, 32
Lowery, Samuel R., 9
lunch-counter sit-ins, *88*, 89

M

Macintosh, Douglas, 41
Madam Foreman (Cooley), 116
Malcolm X, 76
Malone, Dudley, 28
Margolick, David, 106, 115
Marshall, Cecilia Suyat, 75, 82
Marshall, John William, 76, 82
Marshall, Norma, 69
Marshall, Thurgood, *68*, **68–84,** *80*
  as adviser to newly independent African nations, 76, 82
  background, 69–71, 82
  chronology, 82c–83c
  definition of "equal," 75

dissents, 79
  on jury selection, ix
  NAACP legal work, 71–73, 76, 82
  public school landmark desegregation case, 35, 37, 64, 73–75, 82
  reaction to Davis, John W., 45, 46
  Roe v. Wade decision, *128*, 129
  as Supreme Court justice, 69, 77–80, 83, *128*, 129
Marshall, Thurgood, Jr., 75, 82
Marshall, Vivian Burey (Buster), 70, 75, 82
Marshall, William, 69, 72
Mary Ann Folker v. Frederick Folker, 5
Massie, Thomas, 31
Mauro, Tony, 116
McCarthy, Joseph, 46
McCorvey, Norma (Jane Roe), 123–24
McDonald, Julia. *See* Davis, Julia McDonald
McKinny, Laura Hart, 115
McMurry College, 121, 136
McNall, Lura, 3, 4, 9, 12, 14
McNall, Uriah, 3, 14
McNamara, John and James, 24, 32
McVeigh, Timothy, x, 98
Medicaid, 133
Medina, Ernest L., 64, 109–11, 118
Mellon, Andrew, 54
Methodist Church, 121, 127
"monkey trial." *See* Scopes trial
Monopoly (board game), 39
Morgan family, 39, 54; *See also* J.P. Morgan & Company
Morgan Stanley (investment firm), 40
Morgenthau, Robert M., *140*, 141
Movement and the Sixties, The (Anderson), 93
"Mrs. Lockwood's Bill," 7, 9, 14
Mr. Smith Goes to Washington (film), 54
murder cases
  Bailey defense tactics, 104–9
  Darrow defense tactics, 20–21, 25–27
  Fairstein prosecution, 139, *147*, 148–50, 152
  spousal, 98, 102–3, 104–6, 114–17
  See also specific cases
Murray, Donald, 71
My Lai massacre, 64, 109–11, 118
My Life as a Radical Lawyer (Kunstler), 94, 99

N

NAACP. *See* National Association for the Advancement of Colored People
NARAL. *See* National Abortion Rights Action League
Nasair, El Sayyid, 98
National Abortion Rights Action League (NARAL), 136
National Association for the Advancement of Colored People (NAACP), 35, 45, 46, 70–73, 82

159

Index